P9-BBV-922

EVEN THE
PROPHET
STARTED OUT AS A
DEACON

EVEN THE
PROPHET
STARTED OUT AS A
DEACON

The Power of Your
Aaronic Priesthood Ordination

SHANE BARKER

ᐱᐱᐱ®

DESERET
BOOK
SALT LAKE CITY

© 2010 Shane R. Barker

All rights reserved. No part of this book may be reproduced in any form or by any means without permission in writing from the publisher, Deseret Book Company, P. O. Box 30178, Salt Lake City, Utah 84130. This work is not an official publication of The Church of Jesus Christ of Latter-day Saints. The views expressed herein are the responsibility of the author and do not necessarily represent the position of the Church or of Deseret Book Company.

DESERET BOOK is a registered trademark of Deseret Book Company.

Visit us at DeseretBook.com

Library of Congress Cataloging-in-Publication Data
Barker, Shane R.
    Even the prophet started out as a deacon : the power of your Aaronic priesthood ordination / Shane Barker.
        p. cm.
    Includes bibliographical references and index.
    ISBN 978-1-60641-820-8 (paperbound)
    1. Aaronic Priesthood (Mormon Church)   2. Mormon boys—Religious life.
I. Title.
    BX8659.5.B36 2010
    248.8'3208889332—dc22   2010022028

Printed in the United States of America   8/2012
Alexander's Print Advantage, Lindon, UT

30   29   28   27

For Marcus and Brady

CONTENTS

EVEN THE PROPHET STARTED OUT AS A DEACON . . . 1

1. RACING THE IRONMAN
   The Power of Your Aaronic Priesthood Calling 5

2. SKI PATROL ON THE WAY
   The Power of Preparation 21

3. RUNNING WITH THE BALL
   The Power of Magnifying Your Calling 36

4. HEY, SNOOPY'S NOSE IS MISSING
   The Power of Your Quorum 52

5. BASEBALL, WRESTLING, AND BACKPACKING
   The Power of Being a Deacon 69

6. THE SMALLEST MAN IN THE BOOK OF MORMON
   The Power of Being a Teacher 86

7. SEEING ANOTHER EAGLE FLY
   The Power of Being a Priest 105

CONTENTS

8. FLY FISHING, CINNAMON ROLLS,
AND ROCK 'N' ROLL
The Power of Preparing for Your Mission 121

9. HOW TO CLEAN A CAMPSITE
The Power of Leadership 140

10. WINNING GAMES AND ROCKING PHILISTINES
The Power of the Aaronic Priesthood. 159

SOURCES 173

EVEN THE PROPHET
STARTED OUT AS A DEACON

"Bishop Reese used to play football?"

Twelve-year-old Robbie scrunched his nose as he tried to picture it. "*Our* bishop? You're kidding!"

Brother Johnson, the deacons quorum adviser, nodded. "He was pretty good, too, from what I understand."

The roomful of deacons exchanged doubtful glances as they thought about it. Bishop Reese was a wonderful man and an inspired leader, and every young man in the room respected and admired him. But their beloved bishop in helmet and pads, tackling running backs and dashing for touchdowns, was difficult to imagine.

Brother Johnson laughed. "What? You don't think Bishop Reese was ever young? Believe it or not, he used to be a kid. There was a time when he was a deacon, just like you are."

Wow! That's quite a thought, but it's true for you, too. As difficult as it might be to imagine, your bishop was once twelve years old. So were your father, your Young Men's president, your stake president. Every priesthood leader you've ever had was once the same age you are, and he was once a member of the Aaronic Priesthood.

Even the *prophet* started out as a deacon!

You see, one of the most exciting blessings of holding the Aaronic Priesthood is that it's preparing you for even bigger things. It's preparing you to serve a mission. It's preparing you to become a worthy husband and father. And it's preparing you for service and leadership in the Church, too.

The next time you're in quorum meeting, take a good look at the young men sitting around you. There's an excellent chance that one of them will one day be a bishop. One of them might be called to be a stake president or a mission president or a general authority. Those young men will one day be home teachers, Sunday School teachers, Scoutmasters, husbands, and fathers.

And so will you!

Remember, the prophet was once a deacon. He was once a teacher, a priest, and an elder. He once sat in quorum meetings just like you do. He took advantage of his opportunities, magnified his priesthood callings, learned the gospel, prepared himself, and gained experience. And when he was prepared for each new step, Heavenly Father called him to new and weightier responsibilities.

The question is, Are you following his example? Are you making the most of your callings and experiences? You see, you never know what great things your Heavenly Father has in store for you. The only question is, Will you be ready for them when he needs you? President Gordon B. Hinckley was. President Thomas S. Monson was. And you can be too. That's what this book is about. It's about magnifying your Aaronic Priesthood callings and taking advantage of your opportunities to build your spiritual muscles so that you'll be ready when the Lord needs you. And for whatever he needs you to do.

Yes, the prophet started out as a deacon. And so have you. Whether you're still the newest deacon in the ward, a seasoned teacher, or a priest preparing for your mission, you are—like the prophet at your age—preparing for even greater, more exciting experiences.

Are you up for the challenge?

Great!

Let's get started.

RACING THE IRONMAN
The Power of Your
Aaronic Priesthood Calling

"Good afternoon, Scouts!"

Four hundred supercharged Boy Scouts roared back at the top of their lungs, "Good afternoon, Shane!"

"Is everyone having fun?"

"Yes!"

"Are you ready to *ruuuummble?*"

"YES!"

My heart was pounding as the Scouts yelled and cheered. It was our last day at Boy Scout camp, and we were wrapping up our camp Olympics. We'd spent the afternoon racing from one zany contest to another, and we were about to run my favorite event, the Ironman Relay.

The rules were simple. One Scout from each troop swam as fast as he could across the camp lake to tag a teammate on the other side. The second Scout then raced around the shoreline to tag a third Scout. That Scout hopped into a canoe and paddled back across the lake to the finish line.

It was an awesome race—fun to watch and exciting to be a part of.

As the swimmers lined up along the edge of the water, a thirteen-year-old Scout named Wyatt caught my eye. He was grinning excitedly, holding up a finger as if to say, "I'm number one!"

I gave him a quick thumbs-up, eager to see him race. I'd gotten to know Wyatt pretty well over the past week, discovering that he was an incredible young man. He wasn't just a good Scout—he actually *radiated* enthusiasm. He was so full of energy and excitement that he energized people just by being around them.

A couple of days earlier I'd asked him to give a talk at a special honor campfire. With no hesitation, he flashed his braces and said, "Sure!"

I knew then that I'd picked the right Scout for the job. And he didn't disappoint me. He told the story of Helaman's stripling warriors and then recited what he called the Top Ten Ways to Follow Their Example. I lost track of the people who later asked if I had a copy of his talk.

I knew he was excited to race in the Ironman. He'd checked with me a dozen times to be certain he understood the race and to make sure he knew exactly what the rules were. He was determined to win.

I waited until the racers were all in their places and then raised my hands.

"Ready . . . spaghetti . . . *go!*"

Thirty Boy Scouts leaped into the lake and began splashing for the far shore. The racers were swimming furiously, but after several seconds a small Scout was overcome by the cold water and panicked. The Scouts were wearing life jackets, so he wasn't in any real danger. But he began flailing at the water and calling for help. Lifeguards spotted him and began rowing toward him.

And that's when Wyatt took action. Giving up the race, he swam to the frightened Scout, taking him by the shoulders and speaking quietly to calm him down. He stayed with the Scout until the lifeguards arrived and pulled him into their rowboat.

By then most of the swimmers had reached the far shore and tagged their partners. Wyatt was so far behind that his team had no chance of winning. But as soon as he was certain the young man was safe, he turned and finished his leg of the race anyway.

When I ran into him later, I took him aside and said, "Wyatt, that was the most unselfish thing I've ever seen. You showed a whole camp full of people what Scouting's all about."

Wyatt just shrugged and said, "The race wasn't the most important thing happening out on the lake today."

Wyatt didn't know it, but he had affected more than one frightened Scout in the water that day. He had made an impact on me too. I knew that I'd seen a real-life hero in action. And I remember thinking that I wanted to be a leader who inspired people the way Wyatt had inspired me.

When I got back to my cabin that night, I wrote about Wyatt's heroism in my journal. I pulled out his Top Ten List (yes, I'd asked for a copy too!) and pinned it on the wall. And I made a list of goals. I resolved that very night to do everything I could to be a better, stronger, more inspiring leader.

As a matter of fact, it's because of Wyatt—and because of other young men like him, young men like *you*—that I wrote this book.

Now, you hold the Aaronic Priesthood. You already know that the priesthood is the power and authority of God. You also know that it's the power by which he created the heavens and the earth.

The exciting thing is that you can use that priesthood to make a difference in this world. You can use that priesthood to bless the lives of others. Through your example, your leadership, and the quality of your life, you can bless, motivate, energize, and inspire everyone around you.

"How can I do *that?*" a young man once asked. "I'm just a kid!"

Just a kid?

Remember that David was just a kid—a simple shepherd boy—when he walked onto a plain to face Goliath. Jesus was only twelve when he astonished the doctors in the temple. Joseph Smith was only fourteen when he walked out of a grove of trees a prophet. Mormon was just sixteen when he was called to command the Nephite army.

And that's just for starters. Remember Helaman's stripling warriors? Those incredible young men—perhaps teenagers, just like you—went up against one of the most ferocious, savage armies ever to take up the sword.

Teenagers!

But they weren't ordinary teenagers—they were young men brimming with the power of righteousness. They marched into battle with such faith, strength, and conviction that they frightened the enemy into surrendering.

Did you catch that? They actually *frightened* the Lamanites into giving up! Take a look at Alma 56 for the whole story.

Don't *ever* underestimate the power of being a kid! Remember that being young is a blessing. As a young man you have energy and vitality that older people often lack. Along with the power of the Aaronic Priesthood, you can use those gifts of energy and vitality to make an impact on the world around you.

Being young is a blessing. Along with the power of the Aaronic Priesthood, you can use your gifts of energy and vitality to make an impact on the world around you.

Speaking to young men, Elder Robert D. Hales said, "Although you do not remember it, you enlisted in this cause with a single decision, made long ago in our premortal existence. There, in the Grand Council in Heaven, you decided to obey the will of your Heavenly Father and His Son, Jesus Christ. Remember this: you are a son of God who decided to follow the Savior when it mattered most, and that makes you a great man indeed" ("To the Aaronic Priesthood," 48).

You see, in the battle for righteousness you've already made your mark. You strapped on your armor, so to speak, and stood beside Jesus. You so proved yourself in premortality that your Heavenly Father held you in reserve for six thousand years—waiting until the battle between good and evil was at its most critical stage—before sending you to earth.

And now's your chance to prove yourself again. In the book of Abraham, the Lord said, "And we will prove them herewith, to see if they will do all things whatsoever the Lord their God shall command them" (Abraham 3:25).

Now is your chance to prove that you will do everything the Lord expects of you. Now is your chance to magnify your priesthood and to make a difference in the lives of others.

As the First Presidency and the Quorum of the Twelve Apostles have said: "You live in a day of great opportunities and challenges—a day in which the priesthood has been restored. You have the authority to administer the ordinances of the Aaronic Priesthood. As you prayerfully and worthily exercise that authority, you will greatly bless the lives of those around you" (*Fulfilling My Duty to God*, 5).

You have been called to make a difference in the world.

Wow!

You have been called to be a wonderful force for good.

And you can be! As a member of the Aaronic Priesthood, you are entitled to the help of your Heavenly Father. You are entitled to the help of angels. You have the power to blaze through life with the energy of a whirlwind and to have the power of the priesthood manifest through you.

I have a young friend named Jason who was playing baseball one day with his friends. A young man named Devin was pitching when a line drive shot straight back from the bat, striking him in the face. Devin dropped like a rock.

"Devin!"

His friends dropped their gloves and ran for the pitcher's mound. Devin was lying flat on his back, breathing but unconscious.

Jason took one look and then looked frantically around the park. A couple of men were coaching a team of ten-year-olds on a nearby field.

Jason pointed.

"Steve, run over there and get those guys right now!"

Steve took off like a rocket. Jason knelt beside his injured friend and said a quick prayer, his eyes filling with tears.

A moment later the two coaches ran up, one of them speaking rapidly into a cell phone. The other man knelt beside Jason.

"Stand back," the man said to the young men crowding around. "Give us some room."

"There's an ambulance on the way," the second man said. "It'll be here in a minute."

Jason nodded but knew there was something more they had to do. He looked at the man kneeling beside him.

"Are you LDS?" Jason asked.

"Yes."

"Then you've got to give him a blessing!"

The coach looked surprised. "Um . . . ah . . ."

"You've got to give him a *blessing*," Jason repeated, a little more firmly. "And you've got to do it now!"

The coach still hesitated, but the second man responded. He knelt beside Devin's head. "C'mon, Ben," he said, "give me a hand."

And then, with the crowd standing around them, the two men placed their hands on Devin's head and used the authority of their priesthood to give him a blessing.

Within minutes a wail of sirens filled the air, and a few minutes later paramedics had Devin on the way to the hospital. It turned out that he was okay—he actually came home from the hospital that same night—but the story wasn't over.

A couple of weeks later Jason's team was picking up

after a game when a man walked up to Jason outside the dugout.

"Do you remember me?" he asked.

"Uh, sorry," Jason said, not recognizing him. "I'm not sure."

"I gave a blessing to your friend a couple of weeks ago."

"Oh, yeah!" Jason said, shaking the man's hand enthusiastically. "I've been wanting to thank you!"

"Actually, I've been wanting to thank *you*."

"Thank *me*? Why?"

"For asking me to give your friend a blessing. I wouldn't have done that on my own. But . . . well, there was something about the way you took charge that day. I felt the Spirit in a way I've never felt it before. And I felt confidence I didn't know I had."

The man paused for a moment before continuing. "I've never experienced anything like that before. And it was incredible. I realized there was something special missing from my life—something I didn't even know was missing until you reminded me."

He put a hand on Jason's shoulder. "I wanted to thank you for blessing my life."

Jason was stunned. He'd only been trying to help his friend. But he, like Wyatt, had made a difference in someone's life without even realizing it.

"We who have been ordained to the priesthood of God can make a difference," President Thomas S. Monson said. "When we qualify for the help of the Lord, we can build boys, we can mend men, we can accomplish miracles in His holy service. Our opportunities are without limit" ("Examples of Righteousness," 65).

You see, you *do* have an influence on the people around you. You *do* make a difference. And just because you don't always see it, don't think for a second that it's not true!

I know a young man named Ryan who was the senior patrol leader of his Scout troop. Ryan was a great leader, but he often worried that he wasn't doing any good. The Scouts in his troop were good kids, but they were typical boys: they were often loud and rowdy during troop meetings and sometimes didn't seem to be paying attention, even during important training.

"It was really discouraging," Ryan told me. "I tried

to make things as fun as I could, but nobody cared. Everything I taught went in one ear and out the other."

What Ryan didn't know was that many of the Scouts *were* listening. One of them was named Travis.

One day Travis was babysitting when his little brother fell through a window. A shard of glass slashed the child's arm, and within seconds it seemed the floor was covered with blood.

Not wasting a second, Travis grabbed his brother's arm and put pressure on the wound. Then he yelled for his sister.

"Quick! Get me a towel! Then call 911!"

Travis took the towel from his sister and clamped it down on the wound, holding it as hard as he could. He kept the wound from bleeding until paramedics arrived and took over.

The paramedics later praised Travis for his quick thinking. They told him he had done everything exactly right and that he had saved his brother's life.

"I just knew what to do," Travis said. "I learned it in Scouts."

Ryan had presented the training in Scouts during a lesson on first aid. He didn't think that anyone was paying attention, but Travis was listening. When his little brother's life was in danger, Travis knew what to do.

Ryan's training saved a life.

The exciting thing is that you never know who is watching you either. You never know who is gaining strength from you, learning from you, or following your example. You never know whose life you're changing.

But rest assured that such people are out there.

The Savior, speaking of the importance of "show[ing] forth good examples," told the sons of Mosiah, "I will make an instrument of thee in my hands unto the salvation of many souls" (Alma 17:11).

President Monson had these thoughts for priesthood holders, young and old: "We have the hearts to serve faithfully in our priesthood callings and thereby inspire others to walk on higher ground and to avoid the swamps of sin which threaten to engulf so many. The worth of souls is indeed great in the sight of God. Ours is the precious privilege, armed with this knowledge, *to make a difference in the lives of others*" ("To Learn, to Do, to Be," 61; emphasis added).

Make a difference in the lives of others! With your

Aaronic Priesthood ordination, you have the power to do that. You have the power to inspire people to be better, to stand taller, and to work harder.

You *can* make a difference!

How to Make a Difference Now!

☑ Think about the example you're setting for people watching you. Is it a good one? Be sure that your example is one that will motivate and inspire others to be better.

☑ Read the story of Helaman's army (Alma 53:18–22; 56:41–56; 57:17–27). Choose one trait of those stripling warriors that would bless *your* life. Make it part of your life, starting today!

☑ Remember that you have been called to make a difference in the world. Think of something you can do to improve yourself, something that will help you to be an even more powerful force for good. Then go do it!

SKI PATROL ON THE WAY
The Power of Preparation

"Seven forty-seven, Summit Patrol."

"Summit Patrol, seven oh-one."

"I need a toboggan and a backboard halfway down Upper Maverick, skiers' right, and I could use an extra patrolman if you can find one."

"Ten-four, Summit Patrol, clear."

"Forty-seven clear."

I released my radio and wiped the snow from my goggles. It was Saturday, and I was working as a ski patrolman in Park City, Utah. My patient was a fourteen-year-old young man named Colby who'd fallen on a steep hillside. He had a broken arm and was complaining about pain in his neck and back.

I didn't think that Colby's injuries were serious, but I needed to take every precaution—and that was a problem. It had snowed heavily the night before, and many of the resort's patrolmen were on the upper mountain doing avalanche control. Two gruesome accidents had just occurred on the other side of the resort, and the patrollers at both scenes had called for medical helicopters. Extra patrolmen were dispatched to help and to establish safe landing zones.

And as if that weren't enough, a fight had broken out in one of the lift lines, requiring several patrollers to sort things out.

In short, things were going crazy, and our resources were stretched thin. I had just returned from a call and hadn't even had time to remove my goggles before being dispatched to the scene I was working now.

Colby began to shiver, and I took my coat off to cover him. On top of everything else, we were on a steep hillside covered with moguls. It was going to be tricky loading him onto a backboard and then onto a toboggan. I needed help, and I wondered where dispatch was going to find anyone to help me.

I splinted Colby's arm, trying to keep him still and

comfortable. Then I happened to look uphill, and I felt my heart leap into my throat.

My friend Taylor was skiing expertly down the hill, towing a rescue sled. And swarming around him were six teenagers—junior patrollers—blazing through the moguls like Olympic racers going for the gold.

I choked up as I watched them. These young men, fifteen- and sixteen-year-olds, were part of our patrol-training program. Yes, they were just teenagers, but as they blazed down the hill, I knew the cavalry had arrived. And I couldn't have been any happier if the surgeon general had just skied up to help.

One of them skied up in a spray of powder, popping off his skis and kneeling in the snow beside me. He lifted his goggles onto his forehead.

"We're here," he announced, sounding as business-like as a heart surgeon preparing for a delicate operation. "What do you need us to do?"

With Taylor's help, two of the young men anchored the toboggan while the others helped me place Colby on a backboard. We lifted him onto the sled and strapped him down. And then, as Taylor grabbed the toboggan handles and began taking the sled downhill, the others followed like fighter jets escorting Air Force One.

For me, those six young men were the undisputed heroes of the day. And I had no doubt they would all become outstanding patrolmen.

I've often thought that those junior patrollers were a lot like Aaronic Priesthood holders. Because they were in training, they weren't yet able to respond to accidents by themselves. But they worked and skied alongside adult patrollers, learning skills and gaining experience they'd need to become qualified patrolmen.

In similar ways, the Aaronic Priesthood is preparing you too, which is why it's sometimes known as the preparatory priesthood.

What is it preparing you for?

To receive the Melchizedek Priesthood. To receive the ordinances of the temple. To serve a mission. To take on the most important role you will ever have in this world, which is that of a worthy husband and father.

The Aaronic Priesthood is preparing you to lead, to serve, and to grow spiritually. It's preparing you for marvelous experiences, opportunities, and blessings that will come to you not only in this life but also in all the eternities to come.

And the time for that preparation is now! Not next month or even next week. The time is *now!*

The question is, are you doing your part? Let's make a quick check.

Do you pray every day?

Are you reading the Book of Mormon?

Are you paying your tithing?

Are you living the Word of Wisdom?

Do you keep the Sabbath day holy, do your home teaching, and attend your meetings?

Do you live as your Heavenly Father wants you to live and as you'll teach people to do on your mission?

If you said *yes* to these questions, you're off to a great start. You *are* developing power in your priesthood, and you *are* magnifying your calling.

If you're a Boy Scout, you know the Scout motto: Be prepared. When Lord Baden-Powell, the founder of Scouting, was asked what Scouts should be prepared for, he said, "Why, for any old thing!" (*Boy Scout Handbook,* 562).

As a member of the Aaronic Priesthood, you never

As a member of the Aaronic Priesthood, you never know what challenges you are preparing yourself for. And you never know when your preparation will be needed. In other words, you need to be ready for anything, and you need to be ready all the time.

know what challenges you are preparing yourself for. And you never know *when* your preparation will be needed.

In other words, you need to be ready for anything, and you need to be ready all the time.

When I was a missionary in Japan, we memorized all of our discussions. It took a lot of work, and for me it was easy to forget the lessons I didn't teach every day. So when I needed to know them, I had to take time to brush up on them. And sometimes—especially if we were busy—I wasn't able to review them as well as I should have.

It wasn't a great system.

One evening we were sitting down to teach a lesson I didn't know as well as a great missionary should. I remember saying a quick prayer, asking for help remembering a lesson I wasn't prepared to teach.

I was scared and nervous. And as I sat wishing I'd taken the time to prepare myself, I remembered something the Lord said to Joseph Smith: "If ye are prepared ye shall not fear" (D&C 38:30).

I resolved that very minute to change. And I did. I got up early the next morning and reviewed the entire first discussion, making certain I knew it well enough to teach it perfectly on a moment's notice.

The next morning I did the same thing with the second discussion. And then the third. I reviewed a different lesson every day. And when I'd finished them all, I started over and reviewed them again. I reviewed an entire lesson every day, making certain that I knew every one perfectly and that I would never forget them again.

And what a difference my new program made!

I never again felt the fear of being unprepared. More important, because I knew my lessons so well, I was able to spend less time worrying and more time teaching. Instead of trying to remember the next line, I was able to improve the quality of my lessons. I was able to concentrate on ways to help my investigators and answer their questions and concerns.

One night I was invited to spend a few hours working with one of my zone leaders.

"We're going to visit a couple of really special families tonight," he said. "What lessons can you teach?"

What followed was one of the most wonderful moments of my entire mission. A warm feeling filled me as I looked him in the eye and said, "Elder Warnick, I can teach whatever you need me to."

He was right. The families we visited *were* special. At the first home we were greeted by two beautiful young girls who invited us into the living room. There was a wonderful feeling in the home. Elder Warnick talked with the family for a few minutes, asking how everyone was and if everyone was reading the Book of Mormon.

Then he turned to me and said, "Elder Barker would now like to explain how your family can live together forever."

Every eye in the home turned to me. At that moment I realized that this was what missionary work was all about. It was what I had been preparing myself for. And I was so thankful I was ready.

The Aaronic Priesthood is preparing you too. It is preparing you for service and opportunities you might never expect. And when those experiences come, you need to be ready for them.

Elder M. Russell Ballard once said in general conference: "You young men who are here tonight need to prepare now for your future service. I would ask, which one of you . . . may someday sit here in the Tabernacle in these red chairs on the rostrum? As unlikely as it may seem to you young men tonight, all of the General Authorities were boys once, much like you. Even I was your age once. No young man should aspire to a calling, but as surely as you are sitting in this priesthood meeting tonight, many of you will preside over wards, stakes, missions, quorums, and, of course, your own families. Priesthood training, my brethren, starts when a young man is ordained a deacon in the Aaronic Priesthood. You Aaronic Priesthood bearers need to understand that you are in training" ("Prepare to Serve," 41).

A few years ago the Scouts in my ward invited me to go camping with them. During the night, a young man named Riley woke me up.

"Brother Barker," he said, "I'm really sick."

Riley was a great kid and I was instantly concerned. He sometimes cut my grass—just because he's a good kid—and he often played with my dog—just because she's a good dog. I figured he had come to me because I know a little first aid. But that wasn't it.

"Would you please give me a blessing?"

"Yeah, sure, Riley."

I made sure Riley was comfortable. Then I woke up one of the Scoutmasters to assist me. Together we used the power of the priesthood to give Riley a blessing.

Afterward, we wrapped Riley back up in his sleeping bag, and within a few minutes he was asleep again.

But I was too keyed up to go back to bed. I kept thinking over and over how glad I was that I was there to help and that I was ready and worthy to give him a blessing.

You see, in a moment of crisis—when the chips are down and you need your Heavenly Father's help—the time for preparation is past. There's no way I wanted to say, "I'd love to help you, Riley, but I just need a couple of days to talk to the bishop and straighten out a few things first!"

I would have felt miserable turning my young friend away because I wasn't prepared.

Elder Jeffrey R. Holland said: "Young men, you will learn, if you have not already, that in frightening, even perilous moments, your faith and your priesthood will demand the very best of you and the best you can call down from heaven. . . . All priesthood bearers must

31

be instruments in the hand of God, and to be so, you must, as Joshua said, 'sanctify yourselves.' *You must be ready and worthy to act*" ("'Sanctify Yourselves,'" 39; emphasis added).

And Elder Ballard made these suggestions: "I say to you young men tonight, get ready; every one of you, get ready. This world needs your service. Repent if you need to. Study from the standard works every day. Say your prayers morning and night. Develop in your heart a *desire* to know the mysteries of God. To lead the Church tomorrow, you must prepare today. Train hard, boys, and I promise you that you will live to be grateful that you made the effort to prepare" ("Prepare to Serve," 42).

I know a young man named Landon. When he was ten, he began noticing the deacons in his ward, realizing that he'd soon be one of them. So he began watching them—closely. He quickly learned the patterns they used for passing the sacrament. He answered the door when they collected fast offerings so he could see what they did and how they acted.

Landon knew there was a connection between deacons and Scouts, so he began working even harder in Cub Scouts, earning all the pins and badges he could.

By the time he turned twelve, Landon had prepared himself to become a deacon. But he didn't stop there. He began watching the teachers, learning what they did. And later he turned his attention to the priests and to returned missionaries. Landon went the extra mile to be sure he was as ready as possible for every stage of the Aaronic Priesthood.

You can do that too. You don't have to wait to become a teacher or a priest or a missionary to prepare for those opportunities. You can start now. In addition to following the counsel given by Elders Holland and Ballard, you can simply do your best in all your priesthood responsibilities. Pay attention in quorum meetings. Participate in activities. Help out in service projects. Work hard in Scouting. Start now to earn your Duty to God certificate and your Eagle Scout Award.

Remember that everything you do in the Aaronic Priesthood has a spiritual purpose and will help prepare you for opportunities and challenges to come.

Remember that your Heavenly Father needs you. He has given you the Aaronic Priesthood to build your spiritual muscles and to give you spiritual experiences. Make the most of your opportunities!

Prepare yourself now for the work your Heavenly Father has planned for you, and the blessings you'll receive will be greater than you could ever imagine.

How to Make a Difference Now!

☑ To truly prepare yourself, you should do such things as pray, study the scriptures, and live the Word of Wisdom every day. Make a special effort to keep those activities part of your daily routine.

☑ Be sure to pay your tithing, attend your meetings, and live as your Heavenly Father expects you to. In order to teach gospel principles as a missionary, you need to live them now.

☑ If you haven't begun working on your Duty to God certificate, start now. Ask your priesthood adviser for a copy of *Fulfilling My Duty to God: For Aaronic Priesthood*

Holders. Do one thing *today* to get started on the requirements!

☑ Do the same thing for your Eagle. Choose a date for completing it. Make a plan. Do one thing *today* that gets you closer to earning your Eagle.

RUNNING WITH THE BALL
The Power of Magnifying Your Calling

"Jake, I hate to do this to you, but I'm stuck. I just don't know what else to do."

Seventeen-year-old Jacob shrugged. "It's fine, Shane," he said. "Quit worrying about it; just tell me what you want me to do."

I sighed and nodded. It was Monday, and we were at Boy Scout camp. It was our first day of summer camp, and within minutes hundreds of excited, energetic Scouts would begin flooding the camp. I was the camp program director, and I wanted our first day to be perfect.

And it would have been too. But a few minutes earlier I'd learned that my pioneering director had accepted another job. And that left me in a bind. The only person able to take over the program was Jake—one of my best lifeguards.

Jake was a great kid and a good friend, but I knew he had his heart set on being a lifeguard. He'd worked hard to prepare himself, taking CPR and lifesaving classes and even joining a swim team to become better in the water. I knew that moving from the lake to a dry, dusty meadow at the top of camp would be disappointing.

"Thanks, Jake," I said. "And listen—the second I can find someone to take over, I'll have you back at the waterfront working on your tan."

He laughed and punched me in the shoulder. "Shane, it's *fine*. I'll do whatever you need me to."

"Okay," I said. I glanced over the coils of ropes and stacks of pioneering poles littering the ground and then pointed across the meadow. "Actually, I've always wanted to have some kind of pioneering tower over there. You know, a huge Boy Scout kind of thing covered with flags and streamers. If you got the Scouts working on it—you know, a little bit at a time—you could probably have one up in a couple of days."

"Yeah, that sounds cool," Jake said. "I'll take care of it."

And I knew he would. The week before, he'd been helping to build a fence around the lake when it started to rain. Everyone else went running for cover, but Jake kept working—rainwater pouring off his hat—until he had finished. He was one of the most dependable young men I knew.

I felt better as I left and hiked down the hill. It was hard juggling staff members around so that they all had the job they wanted, and I appreciated Jake for being so willing to help out in a pinch. I hoped he'd be as excited about building a tower as I was. Other than burned pancakes and messy campsites, there's nothing as symbolic of Boy Scout camping as a good old-fashioned pioneering tower. And having one there in the meadow would be just the touch our camp needed.

I figured it would take a couple of days to get it finished. But a couple of hours later I walked up the hill to see how Jake was doing. I walked around the corner and saw an enormous tower in the middle of the meadow. Scouts were scrambling over it like monkeys, checking lashings and tying on colorful streamers that snapped in the breeze. A huge American flag waved from a pole lashed to the top.

I stopped and stared in amazement and then went looking for Jake.

"Hey, Shane!" he called from a pile of rope he was sorting. "You like it?"

"Yes, I like it! It's . . . I mean . . . Jake, it's *awesome!*"

He grinned proudly. "Looks cool, huh? We've been having a great time with it."

I couldn't believe what he'd accomplished since morning. In addition to those working on the tower, Jake had Scouts tying knots, splicing ropes, lashing poles, and completing other requirements for rank advancement and the pioneering merit badge. The place was a beehive of activity as Scouts lashed, tied, and knotted every rope and pole in sight. I knew already that for many Scouts, pioneering would be the highlight of their week.

A lot of people in Jake's position—disappointed at being moved from a more glamorous job at the lake—would have sulked. But not Jake. Like a football player intercepting a pass, he took the ball and ran with it. He took his job and did the very best he could with it, turning a dull assignment into a roaring adventure. He invented games, contests, and challenges, sparking everyone's imagination and turning a humdrum area into an adventure land that drew Scouts like a magnet.

Jake eventually got to return to the lake. But before he did, he turned our pioneering area into one of the most explosive, exciting programs in camp.

Now, you are a member of the Aaronic Priesthood, and you are expected to magnify your callings. Whether you're the greenest deacon in the Church or a priest making an appointment for a missionary haircut, you're expected to fulfill the responsibilities of your priesthood office.

There are a lot of big words in that last paragraph. But what do they mean? *Magnify your calling* simply means doing your best in it. Your *very* best.

You see, when you fulfill your duties to the best of your ability, you become better at them. And the better you become, the more you'll be able to accomplish. Your abilities will grow, expand, and *magnify.*

Doing his best is what Jake did at Scout camp. And that's what you can do with your assignments in the priesthood.

I know a young man named Tanner who was called to be president of his teachers quorum. The first thing he did was sit down with his counselors and say, "Lance hasn't come to church in a long time. And Matt comes only once in a while. What do you think we ought to do about that?"

Tanner next made an appointment with the elders quorum president to make sure everyone in the teachers quorum had home teaching assignments—even the less-active ones.

And he was just getting started. He invited a returned missionary to talk in priesthood meeting about preparing for missions. With his counselors he visited every member of the quorum, hoping to learn more about each young man in order to better meet his needs.

He began reading the Book of Mormon—again. He scheduled regular meetings with his priesthood adviser, asking for help and suggestions in leading the quorum.

Tanner didn't simply sit back and let his adviser take charge and do all the work. Instead, he took the bull by the horns and tried to be the best quorum president he could be. He truly magnified his calling.

And you can do the same thing. You can do the best you can with the jobs you're given, preparing yourself for even greater responsibilities later.

I have a friend named Hal who's a junior high school teacher.

"A couple of years ago my work slipped into a rut," he once told me. "My classes were dull and boring, and I knew I needed to put a little more *zing* into my work."

"So what did you do?" I asked him.

"I made a plan. I decided that every day I'd go to work and find one thing I could do better that day. And then I'd do it."

"Just one thing?"

"Just one thing—every single day."

Wow, I thought. By the end of the school year he'd have a hundred and eighty new ideas energizing his classroom. Can you imagine the spark that put into his classes?

Now imagine yourself using an approach like that to magnify your priesthood callings. Suppose you decided that every week—or every month—you'd do one new thing to improve your spirituality, build your testimony, or prepare for your mission.

One week, for instance, you might begin reading the Book of Mormon every day. The next week you might set a date to complete your Eagle and then make a schedule for following through.

Can you imagine what a goal like that would do for you? Can you imagine the direction—and motivation—it would give you?

How could you *not* be successful with a program like that? You'd blaze into your mission with the power of a rocket!

I once heard a motivational speaker give a talk about water.

Water?

"At 211 degrees, water's pretty hot," he said. "And it's good for mopping floors or washing your socks. But at 212 degrees that water begins to boil. So by increasing the temperature by one degree—just *one* degree—that hot water begins to produce steam. And it is suddenly able to generate electricity. It's able to power locomotives and drive powerful turbine engines."

All that just by increasing the temperature by *one* single degree!

Imagine what *you* might accomplish by improving yourself by one degree. Like hot water beginning to boil, that single degree could transform you from an outstanding young man into a rock-'em, sock-'em, razzle-dazzle, rip-roaring Aaronic Priesthood bearer able to run faster than a speeding elder and able to leap tall bishops in a single bound!

How do you get started?

Elder Russell M. Nelson gave this advice:

"To magnify your callings in the Aaronic Priesthood, you young men should shape your personal efforts toward five personal objectives to:

- Gain a knowledge of the gospel of Jesus Christ.
- Be worthy of missionary service.
- Keep yourself morally clean and qualified to enter the holy temple.
- Pursue your personal education.
- Uphold Church standards and be worthy of your future companion" ("Personal Priesthood Responsibility," 46).

Imagine what you might accomplish by improving yourself by one degree. Like hot water beginning to boil, that single degree could transform you from an outstanding young man into a rock-'em, sock-'em, razzle-dazzle, rip-roaring Aaronic Priesthood bearer able to run faster than a speeding elder and able to leap tall bishops in a single bound!

Good advice! As a matter of fact, you could use Elder Nelson's suggestions as a get-started checklist. Are you learning the gospel? Are you keeping yourself worthy to serve a mission?

If you are, you're on the right track. And if you're not . . . well, you know what to do!

Another critical step in magnifying your callings is to *learn your duties*. After all, it's impossible to fulfill your priesthood duties if you don't know what they are.

You see, deacons, teachers, and priests all have specific duties to perform. And your Heavenly Father expects you to know what they are. As he said to the Prophet Joseph Smith, "Wherefore, now let every man *learn his duty,* and to act in the office in which he is appointed, in all diligence" (D&C 107:99; emphasis added).

In other words, the Lord expects you to know what your duties in the Aaronic Priesthood are. And then he expects you to go out and do them.

You can start with the Doctrine and Covenants. Deacons, for instance, are told to "watch over the church" (D&C 20:84:111) and "to warn, expound,

THE POWER OF MAGNIFYING YOUR CALLING

exhort, and teach, and invite all to come unto Christ"
(D&C 20:59).

Teachers are called "to watch over the church
always, and be with and strengthen them" (D&C
20:53) and to "see that there is no iniquity in the
church, neither hardness with each other, neither lying,
backbiting, nor evil speaking" (D&C 20:54).

Priests are expected "to preach, teach, expound,
exhort . . . and visit the house of each member, and
exhort them to pray vocally and in secret and attend
to all family duties" (D&C 20:46–47). Priests are also
allowed to perform baptisms, to confer the Aaronic
Priesthood, and to ordain deacons, teachers, and priests
when authorized by the bishop (D&C 20:46, 48).

We'll talk more about these things later. But remember that this isn't a complete list. You might need
to ask your father, grandfathers, quorum advisers,
bishop, teachers, and other leaders for more details.

And remember that you are entitled to personal
revelation too. So as you strive to learn and fulfill the
duties of your callings, don't be afraid to ask your
Heavenly Father for help!

But knowing your duties is just a start. The Lord

expects you to fulfill them "in all diligence." Remember Jake and Tanner? They're examples of young men fulfilling their duties "in all diligence."

Whatever your callings are, dare to do more than the bare minimum. Dare to be better than average. As my mission president once said, "This is your opportunity to rise above mediocre."

Do your best!

Make a difference!

And not just in church.

To become a truly powerful priesthood holder, you need to do your best in school, at home, at work, and in everything you do. Doing your best means taking the gifts and talents your Heavenly Father has blessed you with and making the most of them.

Why?

President Spencer W. Kimball once said, "Even if the priesthood holders of our Heavenly Father are headed in the right direction, if they are men without momentum they will have too little influence. You are the leaven on which the world depends; you must use your powers to stop a drifting and aimless world."

How do you do that? President Kimball told us:

"It is most appropriate for Aaronic Priesthood youth . . . to quietly, and with determination, set some serious personal goals in which they will seek to improve by selecting certain things that they will accomplish within a specified period of time" (*Priesthood*, 5).

So if you have a gift for music, use it! Become better at it! Practice and play and join a choir or a music group if you can.

If you have a gift for sports, join teams, play ball, coach little kids, and learn to officiate.

Do you have a great smile? Then share it with everyone you see. Wear it out! Use it to cheer up and brighten the lives of others.

Remember that the Lord didn't give you those gifts for nothing. He expects you to use them, to share them, to make the most of them, and to bless the lives of others with them.

President Kimball said you must "use your powers to stop a drifting and aimless world." You can do that. You really can! And as you do, you'll make a difference. You'll inspire people. You'll motivate people. You'll encourage them, bless them, and help them just by being around them.

Don't wait until later.
Get started now!

How to Make a Difference Now!

☑ Think of one thing you can do *today* to magnify your priesthood callings. Then do it!

☑ Remember the example of boiling water. Think of something you can do today to increase your spirituality, build your testimony, or prepare you for your mission. And go do it!

☑ Reread President Kimball's counsel on the previous page. Then choose a goal for yourself—a goal that will help you in school, get you closer to your Eagle, or prepare you for your mission. Do one thing today to help you reach that goal.

☑ Take a moment to consider your talents. Choose one of them, and then do one thing to help you become better at it.

Spend an hour practicing, working, painting, or rehearsing—anything to improve your ability. Do it now!

HEY, SNOOPY'S NOSE IS MISSING

The Power of Your Quorum

Ryan was grinning as he walked to the front of the classroom. Ryan was the president of his deacons quorum, and it was his turn to present the priesthood lesson.

"We're going to do something a little different today," he announced, holding out a box with a picture of Snoopy on the front. "I brought a jigsaw puzzle, and Brother Wright said we could spend a few minutes putting it together."

He opened the box and spilled the contents on the floor. He dropped to his knees and looked around. "Well, don't just sit there," he said, "give me a hand!"

He didn't have to ask twice. The deacons were

typical twelve- and thirteen-year-olds, always eager for something to do—even if it was working on a child's jigsaw puzzle.

"Find all the edges first," one jigsaw expert suggested as he sorted through the pieces.

"And the corners," another deacon advised.

"Look, here's part of his tail."

"And here's a piece of his nose. Put it up there at the top."

According to the box, the puzzle was designed for three- and four-year-old children. It contained only about thirty large pieces, so it wasn't long before the young men had finished it. The only problem was that one large piece was missing, right in the middle.

"Way to go, Ryan," someone protested. "You brought a defective puzzle!"

"Oh, I don't know," Ryan said, eyeing the finished product. "It doesn't look *that* bad."

"What are you talking about?" someone asked. "It looks dumb."

"Why?"

"'Cause it's not all there!"

Ryan tried to look surprised. "Is that important?"

"Of *course* it's important! You can't have a puzzle without all the pieces."

Ryan grinned slyly; he had his friends right where he wanted them. He pointed toward the one empty chair in the room. "You might have noticed that Kevin hasn't been to priesthood in a while. So in a way, we're like this puzzle. We're not complete. Without Kevin we're not a whole quorum."

Ryan had made his point. He'd taught his lesson so well that everyone in the room understood it perfectly. And they spent the next several minutes discussing ways to bring Kevin back into activity.

When you received the Aaronic Priesthood, you became a member of a quorum. And no matter where you go, no matter what you do, no matter how old you are, you'll always belong to one.

And *that* is one of the most important blessings of the priesthood.

Why?

Because as a member of a quorum, you'll always have other priesthood holders to help you, support you, and watch over you. You'll always have members

As a member of a quorum, you'll always have other priesthood holders to help you, support you, and watch over you. You'll always have members of the priesthood to give you a hand when you struggle or to throw you a lifeline when you're in trouble.

of the priesthood to give you a hand when you struggle or to throw you a lifeline when you're in trouble.

As the Old Testament preacher said: "Two are better than one; because they have a good reward for their labour. For if they fall, the one will lift up his fellow: but woe to him that is alone when he falleth; for he hath not another to help him up" (Ecclesiastes 4:9–10).

Let me show you how it works.

I know a young man named Michael who began drifting into inactivity. For a while no one thought much about it. But one day the quorum adviser asked, "What's happened to Michael? How come he hasn't been coming to church or to Scouts?"

"I don't know," answered Spencer, the quorum president.

"Don't you think you ought to find out?"

Spencer agreed. He knew Michael well enough to simply ask him what was going on. It turned out Michael didn't have any real problems. He just felt bored at church. His family wasn't active, so there wasn't anyone at home to encourage him. And since he wasn't interested in merit badges or camping, he had no reason to go to Scouts.

When Spencer reported back, his adviser asked, "What are you going to do about that?"

"*Me?* Why *me?*"

"Because you're the quorum president," the adviser said. "You have the keys to preside over the quorum. And as president, you have a special responsibility for less-active members."

With that, Spencer went to work. With the help of his adviser, counselors, and other quorum members, he began coming up with activities Michael would be interested in. He made a point of inviting him to meetings and outings. When Michael went to church, Spencer made sure he had someone to sit with.

But that wasn't all. Spencer also made sure Michael was invited to movies, ball games, and other activities the guys took part in away from church. He made sure Michael knew he was wanted *and* needed. He also made sure Michael knew that the quorum wasn't going to give up on him.

It took some time, but Michael responded. He began attending meetings regularly. And when one of

Spencer's counselors in the quorum presidency moved from the ward, Spencer asked the bishop if Michael could be called to be a counselor in the quorum presidency.

Through that experience, Spencer learned an important lesson about quorums. He learned that even though Michael might lose interest in the quorum, the quorum could never, *ever* lose interest in Michael.

When I was in college I began taking flying lessons. I was making a solo cross-country flight one day, trying to keep my altitude at an even 2,000 feet. After several minutes I looked at my instruments and was amazed to see that I'd drifted up to 2,400 feet.

Man, Kelvin would kill me if he knew, I thought, picturing my by-the-book instructor as I dropped the plane to the correct altitude.

I leveled off at 2,000 feet but was suddenly a few degrees left of course. I corrected my heading but floated up a hundred feet.

You see, keeping an airplane exactly on course takes work. Wind currents are constantly buffeting the plane—pushing it from side to side—while updrafts and downdrafts affect its altitude. A pilot has to make constant adjustments to the plane's heading and altitude to keep it on course.

People are like that too. We're constantly buffeted by trials, temptations, and challenges that can blow us off course. But whenever we begin to drift away, a good priesthood quorum can reach out and bring us back.

What a great blessing!

I belong to the National Ski Patrol. After every snowstorm, patrollers do avalanche-control work, knocking down cornices, making ski cuts, and sometimes even throwing explosives onto slopes to eliminate the possibility of snowslides.

It can be dangerous work, so patrollers have an ironclad rule: they never work alone. Whenever they're doing avalanche control, they *always* have a partner watching out for them. That way, if anyone ever makes a mistake or gets caught in a slide, he has someone looking out for him, ready to call for help or ski to the rescue.

In a very real way, your quorum does the same thing. It watches over you, standing ready to reach out and help if you ever need it. And you, in turn, help to watch out for everyone else.

Is that important?

Of course it is!

"Along your pathway of life you will observe that you are not the only traveler," President Thomas S. Monson said. "There are others who need your help. There are feet to steady, hands to grasp, minds to encourage, hearts to inspire, and souls to save" ("How Firm a Foundation," 68).

Now, it's possible that your quorum isn't operating at 100 percent. If it's not, be sure to do your part anyway. Who knows? You might be the spark the quorum needs to get up to speed.

And if your quorum *is* working well, be sure you do your part to keep it that way.

President Gordon B. Hinckley said: "It will be a marvelous day, my brethren—it will be a day of fulfillment of the purposes of the Lord—when our priesthood quorums become an anchor of strength to every man [young and old] belonging thereto, when each such man may appropriately be able to say, 'I am a member of a priesthood quorum of The Church of Jesus Christ of Latter-day Saints. I stand ready to assist my brethren in all of their needs, as I am confident they stand ready to assist me in mine. Working together, we shall grow spiritually as covenant sons of God. Working together, we can stand, without embarrassment and without fear, against every wind of adversity that might blow, be it economical, social, or spiritual'" ("Welfare Responsibilities of the Priesthood Quorums," 86).

When I was an assistant Scoutmaster, my troop once built a tower out of pioneering poles. Afterward, as we sat on top eating pizza, our Scoutmaster said, "You know, we all worked together to build this tower. It took all of us to do it. But now that it's built, *it's* supporting *us.*"

He looked around, making sure we were getting the message. "You need to understand that our deacons quorum is like this tower. It takes all of us to make a quorum. But the purpose of our quorum is to support us. It's to support you and you and you."

Yes, your quorum can be a great blessing. But it only works if you do. And you have the power to turn a good quorum into a great quorum.

How do you do that?

Let's look at a few ideas.

PARTICIPATE IN ACTIVITIES

A trip to the art museum may not be your idea of fun. But if that's what the quorum or Scout group has planned, go anyway. After all, it's not the activity that's important. It's the fact that you're together as a quorum.

The thing is, you never know when someone might be hurting or going through a bad time. Your friendship—your companionship—might be the very thing that person needs that night. You might provide the spark he needs to snap himself out of his slump. You never know when something you do or say will bless, strengthen, or inspire one of your friends.

So go! Participate! Share your energy and enthusiasm. Do everything you can to make every activity an outrageous success!

PARTICIPATE IN QUORUM MEETINGS

Okay, you've heard the lesson before. And you know how the story ends. But that's no reason to put your feet up and go to sleep.

If you've ever taught a lesson, you know how much better it is when everyone participates. So do your part to help when someone else is teaching. Ask questions. Volunteer answers. Share your thoughts, opinions, and experiences. Help make the lesson a discussion rather than a lecture. Do your part to make every meeting more interesting.

Remember that gaining deep, doctrinal insights is not really the point of most meetings. You're there to grow *spiritually,* to learn from one another, and to share testimonies. And you can't do that if you're doodling in the back of the room.

SUPPORT YOUR QUORUM PRESIDENCY

I was once talking with a young man named Andrew, who was president of his teachers quorum.

"I'm in charge of a service project after school today," he said. "And I'm worried no one's gonna be there."

"Really? Why not?"

"Well, a couple of the guys play baseball, and they've got games tonight. And Nick's in a play or something."

He shook his head. "I'm worried that I'll be the only one who shows up."

I felt bad for Andrew. But when I asked him how it went the next day, his eyes lit up like a Christmas tree.

"It was great! Most of the guys actually showed up early, and we had the whole thing done in less than an hour!"

The day might come when *you* are called to serve in your quorum presidency. When it does, you'll appreciate guys who support you and who are enthusiastic about the lessons and activities you plan for them.

So in the meantime, be supportive and enthusiastic for *your* leaders. Make their job easier by being teachable and submissive. Be excited about outings and activities, and do your best to make them successful.

BUILD QUORUM UNITY

An eighth-grader named Zach once invited me to watch a baseball game he was playing in. He started in left field, but after a couple of innings the coach sent him in to pitch.

Atta boy, I thought as he jogged out to the mound.

I knew that he'd never pitched in an actual game before, and I knew he was excited but nervous.

As the umpire called "batter up!" the greatest thing happened. All the other infield players ran up to the pitcher's mound and took turns slapping Zach on the back and wishing him luck.

Wow, I thought, watching Zach's grin widen. *That's awesome!*

Even from the bleachers I could see his confidence building, and I knew he was lucky to have such great teammates.

Now imagine a member of your quorum preparing to give a talk in sacrament meeting or rappel off a cliff at Scout camp. Imagine him preparing to do anything that might be hard, scary, or out of his comfort zone. And imagine the rest of the quorum—like Zach's teammates—showing their support and encouragement.

Can you imagine the confidence he would feel?

Can you imagine the confidence *you* would feel?

Helping and supporting one another is one of the most important duties of quorum members. So help out! Do your part to build quorum unity. And if you're part of your quorum presidency, look for activities that will help bind the quorum together.

President Henry B. Eyring said: "One of the hallmarks of a strong quorum is the feeling of fellowship among its members. They care for each other. They help each other. Quorum presidents can build that fellowship best if they remember the Lord's purpose for unity in the quorum. It is of course so that they will help each other. But it is more, much more. It is so that they will lift and encourage each other to serve in righteousness with the Master in His work to offer eternal life to Heavenly Father's children."

President Eyring continued, saying: "My prayer is that you will accept the Lord's invitation to become united, as one, in our quorums of the priesthood. He has marked the way. And He has promised us that with His help good quorums can become great quorums. He wants that for us. And I know that He needs stronger quorums to bless the children of our Heavenly Father. . . . I have faith that He will" ("Priesthood Quorum," 44–45).

As you progress through the Aaronic Priesthood, your quorum can be one of your greatest blessings. It can be a lifeline when you're in trouble. It can be an anchor when you drift. It can be the boost you need whenever you feel lost, lonely, or discouraged.

And you, in turn, can be the lifeline, the anchor, the boost, or the spark for others.

You really do have the power to make your quorum awesome! *You* can be the spark that ignites and energizes the entire quorum, helping everyone to magnify their callings and realize their potential.

So don't wait another second! Resolve now to participate in every meeting. Decide now to take part in every activity. Support your quorum leaders and do everything you can to build quorum unity.

Your Heavenly Father will bless you as you do. And you'll make a difference more powerful than you can ever imagine!

How to Make a Difference Now!

☑ Whatever activity your quorum has planned this week, be sure that you go! Then do your part to make it successful. Be happy and enthusiastic! Use your friendship and personality to make the activity more fun for everyone.

☑ Decide now that you'll sit on the front row in your next quorum meeting. Then be sure to participate! Resolve now to make a comment, ask a question, or share an experience. Be sure to do *something* to make the meeting better for everyone.

☑ Think of someone in your quorum who could use a compliment, a smile, or a word of encouragement. You don't need to do anything big, but think of *something*. Then do it! Offer a compliment or a smile. Or write a note instead. Do *something* to bless the life of someone in your quorum and remind him that he's special.

BASEBALL, WRESTLING, AND BACKPACKING

The Power of Being a Deacon

Brady and Cole were tossing a baseball back and forth behind the dugout.

"Your arm feeling okay?" I asked Brady as I watched.

He nodded, catching the ball and putting a little snap into his throw to Cole. "Feels great, Coach."

"Good and loose? No tightness or anything?"

"No, feels great, Coach."

"Okay. Keep it nice and easy for a bit; you need to save your arm for the game."

"Got it."

I watched the young men for another second, glad they were playing for me and not for the other team.

We were nearing the end of the season and were about to play our biggest rivals, the Yankees. We'd never played them, but I knew they had a strong team and a good record. Brady was one of the best pitchers in the city, but he'd have to throw his very best stuff to win this one.

I watched him make another throw, and then I turned for the dugout.

"Hey, Coach?"

"Yeah?"

"Can I ask you something?"

"Sure," I said. "What is it?"

Brady slapped the ball into his glove, looking suddenly serious. He gestured across the field to where the Yankees were busy throwing to one another.

"There's a kid named Steve over there. Cole and I know him from school."

"Yeah?"

"He's not very good," Cole said, walking over to join us. "He's cool and everything, but he's not very athletic, and the other kids give him a hard time about it."

"Uh-huh."

"Well," Brady said, "Cole and I were wondering if we could let him get a hit tonight."

"You what?"

"He'll probably only get to bat once or twice," Brady continued. "Would you mind if I took a little heat off my pitches when he's up? Maybe give him something he can hit?"

I looked at Brady for a moment and then glanced at Cole. They were watching me expectantly, and I could tell this wasn't a random question; they'd put a lot of thought into it.

"You're serious, aren't you?"

They nodded.

Wow, I thought. I appreciated them for having the courtesy to ask permission. And I knew they'd respect my decision if I said no. I wasn't going to stop them if they wanted to let their friend get a hit that bad. But I decided to see just how serious they were.

"What if there's someone on base?" I asked. "What if it's a close game and they have a chance to score? If your friend gets a hit, it could cost us the game. Would you still let him hit?"

Brady's eyes just gleamed. "Wouldn't that be cool?"

he asked, looking at Cole. He looked back at me. "You don't know how awesome that would make him feel!"

I hoped it wouldn't come to that, but I told them to go ahead. In the third inning when Steve—looking like a chipmunk facing off against wolves—came up to bat, I was eager to see what Brady would do. We were ahead by a couple of runs, and there was one out.

Brady didn't give any indication that anything was up. He stared down a runner on third for a moment, set his teeth, and then rifled the ball straight down the middle. I could tell he hadn't thrown quite as hard as usual. It was a perfect pitch—the kind batters call *meat*.

And it was just what Steve was looking for.

He swung his bat, smacking the ball past Brady and into a gap in center field. The kid on third ran home as Steve bolted for first. My center fielder swooped down on the ball like a hawk after a mouse, snatching it off the grass and throwing it on the run. It reached first base . . . a split second after Steve.

The crowd went wild. Parents in the stands cheered while players in the Yankee dugout stood and shook the fence. The first-base coach slapped Steve enthusiastically on the back.

As for Steve, I could see the excitement on his face from clear across the field.

Brady looked just as happy. He traded looks with Cole and then turned and glanced at me. He grinned when I gave him a thumbs-up, and I realized that he was more than just a good pitcher. He was a special kid, and I couldn't have been more proud of him if he'd just won the city championship.

But that's the way Brady was. The year before he'd given up a chance to play on a traveling super-league team because it meant playing on Sundays. He could have played in some great tournaments and had a lot of fun, but he knew there were more important things than baseball—just as he knew there were more important things than winning.

Earlier in the season he and Cole had asked if they could skip practice one Friday night to attend a friend's party. I said yes, but about an hour into practice they showed up anyway.

"What's going on?" I asked. "I thought you were going to a party."

"We went," Brady said. "But Rory's parents weren't there. And the guys were going to watch some ranky movie."

"Ranky?"

"The kind kids aren't supposed to watch," Cole explained.

"And so you left."

It wasn't a question, but they nodded anyway. They were both wearing expressions that seemed to say, "What's the big deal? That's what we're supposed to do!"

As they ran to their places on the field, I realized how much I admired them, not just for having high standards but also for living up to them.

When you received the Aaronic Priesthood, you made covenants to live the principles of the gospel. You promised to obey your Heavenly Father's commandments. Brady and Cole lived up to those covenants. And as a deacon, you need to live up to them too.

When you think of being a deacon, you probably think of passing the sacrament and collecting fast offerings. Those are important duties, and we'll talk about them in a moment. But you also have the responsibility "to watch over the church" (D&C 84:111). And you have the duty "to warn, expound, exhort, and teach, and invite all to come unto Christ" (D&C 20:59).

What does that mean?

Let me give you a couple of examples.

Several years ago I met a seventh-grade wrestler named Caleb. He was a gifted athlete with a roomful of trophies. He won nearly every time he wrestled, but he was always compassionate. After every match Caleb made a point of finding his opponent and sitting with him, watching other matches and making friends. He often traded singlets (wrestling uniforms) and e-mail addresses with his new friends and then kept in touch afterward.

At one meet he was matched against a young man named Jeremy, who was wrestling in ordinary gym clothes.

"Don't you have a singlet?" Caleb asked before the match.

Jeremy shook his head. "Our coaches haven't given 'em to us yet."

"Hang on a second."

75

Caleb ran to his gym bag, pulled out a spare singlet, and gave it to Jeremy.

"Have you ever wrestled Danny Williams?" Caleb asked.

"No, but I've watched him," Jeremy said. "He's awesome."

"He is," Caleb agreed. "But I pinned him last year when I was wearing that singlet. I think it's lucky."

That's the kind of young man Caleb was. But he didn't stop there. Caleb made a point of asking his new friends if they were members of the Church. If they said no, he gave them a Book of Mormon that he carried in his gym bag. If they said yes, he asked if they were Scouts and if they were working on their Eagle.

When Jeremy admitted that he wasn't interested in Scouting, Caleb replied, "Big mistake, man. You've gotta get your Eagle. It'll change your life!"

Did Caleb make a difference?

He did to Jeremy! I know because Jeremy told this story the night he received his Eagle.

"When I was twelve I wasn't interested in Scouting," he said during his court of honor. "I was more excited about wrestling than earning merit badges."

And then Jeremy introduced Caleb, who was in the audience. "That changed the day I met Caleb," he said. "He pinned me and then challenged me to earn my Eagle."

Jeremy grinned wryly and added, "He's here tonight to make sure I'm going on a mission!"

You see, Caleb made a point of inviting others "to come unto Christ" (D&C 20:59). He used the power of his friendship to help others improve themselves. He used the power of his example to encourage them to raise their standards and lengthen their strides.

Can *you* do that?

Of course you can!

I once noticed an eighth-grader named Josh giving a *For the Strength of Youth* pamphlet to one of his friends. I wasn't trying to be nosy, but since I don't see that sort of thing every day, I later asked him about it.

"Jason's really into girls," Josh explained. "He's always 'going out' with someone, breaking up, and then 'going out' with someone else. And he doesn't go to church very often. So I reminded him that we have been counseled to wait until we are sixteen to date, and I gave him a pamphlet to help him remember."

I don't know if Jason ever changed his ways, but I was proud of Josh for watching out for his friends.

Let me promise you something: when you make the effort to warn and teach and invite others to come unto Christ, the Lord will bless you. And he'll help you. He'll guide you and give you ideas. You'll learn that you *can* make a difference in this world.

And you *will* make one.

Passing the Sacrament

When I was a Scout, our troop once went backpacking. We had to climb several miles up a steep, rocky trail. I was carrying one of the tents (that I think my tent mate filled with rocks), along with several water bottles that seemed to grow heavier with every mile.

When I finally reached the campsite and dropped my pack, I felt as if the weight of the world had just been lifted from my shoulders. I felt as light as a feather and went bouncing around the campsite as if I had springs in my boots. Five minutes earlier I was ready to drop. But a second after dropping my pack, I felt wonderful, energized, and charged with adrenaline.

I felt *fantastic!*

When people are baptized and forgiven of their sins, they often feel something like that. As the dark weight of sin is lifted from them, they're filled with joy, gratitude, and relief. Taking the sacrament helps people to remember that great experience and allows them to renew their commitment to their Father in Heaven.

"As you Aaronic Priesthood holders assist in preparing, blessing, administering, and passing the sacrament," President James E. Faust taught, "you help all members who partake thereof to recommit themselves to the Lord and to renew their faith in the Savior's atoning sacrifice. Members who take the sacrament are reminded to take upon themselves the name of the Son, always remember Him, keep His commandments, and seek to have His Spirit to be with them. I hope that you will value the priesthood you hold and always honor your priesthood duties" ("Royal Priesthood," 50).

You see, when you pass the sacrament, you're doing more than simply handing out bread and water. You're helping people to perfect their lives.

And you get to participate in that!

How fantastic is that?

Collecting Fast Offerings

A deacons quorum adviser once told me that he always struggles to get enough deacons and teachers to collect fast offerings.

"But there's a deacon named Alec who's there every month—rain or shine," he said. "I never have to remind him. He's always there early, and he doesn't stop until we're finished."

"Good kid, huh?"

"He's a great kid, but there's more to it than that."

"And what's that?"

My friend explained that there was a time when Alec's family had no money. His parents weren't together, and his mother had lost her job. They didn't have a car, and sometimes they barely had enough to eat.

"When their bishop discovered how tough things were, he offered assistance," my friend said, smiling. "Alec *knows* why we collect fast offerings. He knows why it's so important. And nothing in the world is going to stop him from doing his part."

Collecting fast offerings might seem like just

another chore. But when you collect fast offerings, you're helping people—*really* helping people. You're blessing their lives.

Keep that in mind the next time it feels like just another chore.

THE POWER OF BEING A DEACON

You might not remember this, but when you became a deacon, the Aaronic Priesthood was conferred upon you, and then you were ordained to the office of deacon. In other words, you were given the priesthood—the same priesthood as teachers and priests—and then you were ordained.

"I don't get that," my friend James said as we discussed it in mutual back when I was your age.

"Well, it's kind of like going into junior high," our teacher explained.

"It's what?"

"When you graduated from elementary school, you entered junior high, right?"

"Right."

"And you were assigned to the seventh grade."

"Yeah."

"Okay. So you were in junior high—just like all the eighth- and ninth-graders. But because you were in seventh grade, you were limited in the classes you were allowed to take and the activities you were allowed to participate in."

"Ah, okay," James said. "That makes sense."

I've always thought that was a good explanation. As a deacon, you don't have any less priesthood than teachers or priests. But you do have some limitations in what you're allowed to do.

You might think that your duties as a deacon are unimportant, but they're not. When you pass the sacrament, you're helping people to perfect their lives. When you collect fast offerings, you're helping people who are in need. When you pass out fliers, act as a messenger for the bishop, or do any of the other traditional duties of a deacon, you're doing the work of the Church—the work of your Heavenly Father. When you warn, expound, exhort, and teach, you are blessing the lives of others. You are making a *difference.*

As a deacon, you're just beginning your preparation for the Melchizedek Priesthood. So make the most of

When you do any of the traditional duties of a deacon, you're doing the work of the Church—the work of your Heavenly Father. You are blessing the lives of others. You are making a difference.

it. Set your sights high. Use the power of your friend-ship and example to motivate, inspire, and energize your friends. Fulfill your priesthood duties to the best of your ability, and magnify your calling.

As you do, you'll gain momentum and prepare yourself for even greater things to come!

How to Make a Difference Now!

☑ Think of someone you can invite "to come unto Christ" (D&C 20:59). Think of one thing you can do or say that would make a good impression on that person. Go do it!

☑ Remember that you have an influence on your friends. Be sure that you're setting a good example for them—especially those who might be less active in the Church.

☑ As you're passing the sacrament this week, think about what it really means. Think about the sacrifice your Savior made for you. Remember that you're helping people to renew important covenants. You're helping them to perfect their lives. Be sure to conduct yourself in a way that's appropriate for such an important ordinance.

☑ Imagine not having enough money to buy food. Or dress warmly. Or pay bills. As you collect fast offerings, remember that you're helping people who are hungry or needy. And remember the words of the Savior: "Inasmuch as ye have done it unto one of the least of these my brethren, ye have done it unto me" (Matthew 25:40).

THE SMALLEST MAN
IN THE BOOK OF MORMON
The Power of Being a Teacher

The basketball flew through the air, nicking the backboard and rattling once around the rim before dropping through the net.

"Score!"

Fourteen-year-old Nathan pumped a fist as his friend Tucker grabbed the ball and dribbled back to the top of the driveway.

"Sixteen to ten," Nathan announced, "for those of you who are mathematically challenged."

"You haven't won yet," Tucker warned, bouncing the ball in a show-off move. "They don't call me Tucker-Scores-a-Lot for nothing."

"Who calls you that?"

"People who play better defense than you."

Tucker flipped the ball to Nathan.

"Check it."

Nathan bounced the ball back. Tucker caught it and dribbled it a couple of times. Then—like an all-star guard trying to make a highlight reel—he faked left and bolted right. Nathan threw out his hands to block him, but Tucker spun—switching the ball to his left hand—and shot for the basket. Nathan dropped back just as Tucker stopped, jumped, and sent the ball winging toward the basket.

Swish!

"Sixteen–twelve," Tucker announced. "For those of you who are defensively challenged."

Nathan grinned as he scooped up the ball. Instead of dribbling back to the top of the driveway, he held the ball and looked down the street.

"We still playing?" Tucker asked after a moment.

"Just a second," Nathan answered, still looking down the street.

Tucker walked over, making a halfhearted attempt to steal the ball. "What are you looking at?"

Nathan gestured to where an elderly man was

mowing his lawn a few houses away. "Just watch for a second."

Tucker watched. The man finished a trip around his lawn, then turned off his mower, walked to the porch, and sat down in the shade. Tucker shrugged. "Yeah? So?"

"I've been watching him for a couple of minutes," Nathan said. "He can only go one time around the lawn before he has to rest."

"You think he's okay?"

"I dunno. I guess we could ask."

Tucker shrugged. "Why not?"

They took turns dribbling the basketball as they walked down the street and up their neighbor's driveway. Brother Packer smiled when he saw them.

"Hello, Nathan. Hello, Tucker."

"Hi," the young men echoed. They hesitated for a moment. Then Nathan said, "We noticed that it's taking you a long time to mow your lawn. Are you okay?"

"Oh, sure!" Brother Packer said. "I'm fine. It just takes me a little longer than it used to."

"Would you like some help?"

"Oh, no. But thank you for offering."

"No, really," Tucker insisted. "It would only take us a minute."

"Seriously," Nathan said, "if we can't mow your lawn, we'll just go back to playing basketball. And to tell you the truth, Tucker's really not much of a challenge."

Tucker began choking, but Brother Packer laughed and let them finish his lawn. A few days later, Nathan went to talk with the ward Young Men president.

"It might not be any of my business," he said, "but I don't think it's good for Brother Packer to be mowing his lawn. I mean, he can only go one time around the yard before he has to rest, and that can't be good for him. I thought maybe we could do something."

The Young Men president agreed. He had a talk with Brother Packer, and the young men of the ward began taking turns mowing his lawn each week.

Now you're probably wondering what any of that has to do with being a teacher in the Aaronic Priesthood. The answer is simple. You see, teachers are called "to watch over the church always" (D&C 20:53). Watching over the Church includes keeping an eye on friends, neighbors, and family members and then stepping in to help if necessary.

And that's exactly what Nathan did. He noticed when a neighbor was in need and then took time to help.

There was nothing remarkable about what Nathan did. He was simply living up to his priesthood responsibilities. The exciting thing is that you can do the same thing. You too can help watch over the Church, keeping an eye out for people in need and then doing what you can to help.

I know a young man named Simon, for instance, who one day asked a friend what he was getting for Christmas.

"My little brother's getting a mountain bike," Curtis answered proudly.

"Cool. But what are *you* getting?"

Curtis hemmed and hawed a little bit but finally looked around to be sure he wouldn't be overheard and said: "We don't have a lot of money this year. But Chris really needs a bike. I told my mom that if she could get one for him, then she didn't have to get anything for me."

Simon was stunned. He knew that Curtis didn't have a father in his home, but he didn't realize that his family might be facing other challenges too. The moment he got home that night he phoned his quorum adviser.

"Brother Lamb, we have a problem."

"Oh? What's that?"

"I don't think Curtis's family has enough money for Christmas."

"Oh? Why not?"

Simon told him about his conversation with Curtis. Brother Lamb agreed to look into it. He contacted the bishop. In the end, being discreet and without causing any embarrassment, the ward made sure everyone in the family had everything they needed for Christmas.

Like Nathan, Simon noticed when someone was in need. And then he did something about it.

When you think of being a teacher in the Aaronic Priesthood, you probably think about preparing the sacrament. Because the sacrament is so closely related to our Savior's atonement, the sacrament is one of the most sacred ordinances in the Church. Being able to participate in its administration is a great honor and privilege.

Remember that priests bless the sacrament, and deacons pass it to the congregation. But teachers prepare the sacrament, which includes setting the tone for the ordinance.

I know a young man named Christian who one Sunday was preparing the sacrament table. A few of the deacons had arrived early and were in their seats, giggling and poking one another.

Christian listened to them for a while as he worked but then stepped down from the stand.

"Do you know this song?" he asked as he hummed "I Know That My Redeemer Lives." As the younger deacons nodded, he gestured, inviting them to hum along with him. After a moment the deacons were all humming reverently. Then the deacons quorum president, realizing what Christian was doing, stood and walked over.

"Sorry," he whispered. "I won't let it happen again."

Christian smiled and returned to the sacrament table. He hadn't gotten after anyone. He hadn't lectured anyone. But his example had set the tone for the sacrament, which, of course, was the focus of the entire meeting.

As a teacher, you have all the responsibilities of a deacon. But you've progressed a little further and you've gained a little spiritual experience, so you have additional responsibilities. As mentioned already, you are expected to "watch over the church always," but you are also instructed to "be with and strengthen them" (D&C 20:53).

What does that mean? Let me give you an example.

I used to be the program director of a Boy Scout camp. As we were preparing to open camp one summer, a Varsity Scout team asked if there was a service project they could help with.

"Yes, there is," I said. "But it's pretty messy. It won't be a lot of fun."

"That's okay," they assured me. "We'll do whatever you need."

The problem was that several dumpsters had sat neglected over the winter. Raccoons and squirrels had scattered piles of wet, mildewing trash everywhere.

I could tell the Scouts weren't excited about cleaning it up. But they were good sports, tugging on gloves and getting to work. I felt bad about asking anyone to do such awful work, so I pulled on gloves of my own and pitched in.

We'd been at it only a few minutes when there was a bloodcurdling whoop followed by a Scout tearing down the hill.

"There you are!" he shouted, hopping over a log as he ran up. "I took a wrong turn at the swimming pool!"

I didn't recognize the newcomer, but I was instantly glad to see him. He was wearing an ear-to-ear grin, radiating enthusiasm like a Fourth of July rocket and looking as excited as a little kid at Disneyland.

"Hi," he said, walking up and shaking my hand. "I'm Chase. What are we doing?"

I gestured. "We've got to pick up all this gooey stuff and put it back in the dumpsters."

"Coooooooll," Chase said, pulling on his gloves and scanning the garbage. "You gotta love this!"

And then Chase tore into the trash, chattering like a squirrel, telling one zany story after another, and making his teammates laugh as they worked. The effect was magical. Five minutes earlier the Scouts had as much enthusiasm as balloons home teaching porcupines.

But now—as if someone had just recharged their batteries—the Scouts were laughing, joking, and actually having fun as they filled bag after bag with trash.

An ugly chore had suddenly become . . . well, it still wasn't fun, but the young men were *having* fun. And they weren't just enjoying themselves, they were doing a better job too.

What was the difference?

A fourteen-year-old who used the power of a good attitude and a fun-loving personality to strengthen his brethren.

When I was in college I once guided a tour down the Colorado River through the Grand Canyon. For three days straight, rainstorms lashed the river. Passengers who came armed with suntan lotion could have spent most of their time huddling beneath ponchos and cowering under tarps.

The river inside the Grand Canyon is cold anyway, and we usually relied on the hot Arizona sun to keep warm. But on this trip thick, black clouds blocked out the sun. So whenever we smashed our boats through the rapids—splashing tons of ice-cold water over everyone—things could have gotten miserable in a hurry.

But there was a fifteen-year-old named Tim who refused to let the weather ruin the trip. Every morning he went right to the front of the boat where things got the wettest. And as we smashed through the rapids, he'd shout and wave his arms like a bull-riding cowboy at a rodeo.

Once, as the boat crashed down from an enormous wave, another wall of icy water shot up from below. The boat slammed into the wave, and for a second Tim disappeared in the foam. The next second the boat crashed into the wall of water, and tons of ice-cold water poured over us.

Through all of it, I kept seeing Tim grinning from ear to ear and shouting, "More! More! Give us *mooooorrrrre!*"

By the time we were through the rapids and into smooth water again, I was laughing so hard I could barely steer. It didn't matter that the sun wasn't shining. It didn't matter that the water was cold. I was having fun! And so was everyone else. And the reason was Tim. His youthful enthusiasm was so contagious that everyone caught it. He kept the entire group perked up the whole time we were on the river.

You probably know people like Chase and Tim. People who motivate, energize, and *strengthen* everyone around them. People who make tough jobs easier. People who keep their friends going when the day is long and the work is hard. People who help others feel better about themselves. People who make every situation better just by being there.

The question is, are you one of them? Do *you* strengthen the people around you? Or—by moaning, groaning, whining, complaining, and always seeing the worst in things—do you bring people down?

As a teacher in the Aaronic Priesthood—as a teenager full of energy and vitality—you have the power to strengthen the people around you. You have the power to lift their spirits when they're down, cheer them up when they're discouraged, and charge their batteries when they're empty. You have the power to keep them going when there's another hill to climb, another weed to pull, or another meeting to sit through.

You can be the spark that keeps them going for the gold, even when they don't think they can. You can, as the Lord said through Joseph Smith, "succor the weak,

As a teacher in the Aaronic Priesthood—as a teenager full of energy and vitality—you have the power to strengthen the people around you. You have the power to lift their spirits when they're down, cheer them up when they're discouraged, and charge their batteries when they're empty.

lift up the hands which hang down, and strengthen the feeble knees" (D&C 81:5).

You *can* do it, you *should* do it, and you *need* do it.

In my geometry class I had an eighth-grade student named Aaron. He was a great student who was fun to work with. But the best thing about him was his energetic attitude.

"Look how gnarly this is!" I heard him say to a friend one day, stabbing his finger at the illustration of a complicated figure.

"It's a polydeca . . . a polypenta . . ."

"A dodecahedron."

"*That's* it! And we get to calculate its surface area. How cool is that?"

I couldn't help laughing. Rather than looking at his assignment as a chore, Aaron looked at it as a challenge. And a tough geometry problem was suddenly a game. More than that, his enthusiasm spread to the entire class. Instead of moans and groans, the room was crackling with energy. The kids were actually having fun doing *math!*

Believe me when I tell you that one person *can* make a difference!

And you can be that person!

The next time you see people around you losing their energy or enthusiasm, be the one to build them up again. Be the one to encourage them, strengthen them, and keep them going.

Now, watching over and strengthening the Church may seem like a full-time job. (And if you hang around a lot of pessimistic people, it can be!) But there's more. You see, teachers are also expected to "see that there is no iniquity in the church, neither hardness with each other, neither lying, backbiting, nor evil speaking" (D&C 20:54).

Wow!

Tough one!

Several years ago the young men in my ward had an overnight campout. They were promised a weekend of fun and adventure, but Mother Nature had other plans. It started raining the moment we arrived and didn't let up the entire weekend. On top of that, sharp flashes of lightning and booming cracks of thunder kept us all pinned down inside a pavilion with nothing to do.

"This is so stupid," one young man griped as we hunkered against the storm.

"I don't know why we even came," someone else added, throwing a rock into the rain. "How come we can't just go home?"

"Yeah. I've got stuff I could be doing!"

"Do you guys know who the smallest person was in the Book of Mormon?"

Silence.

The question was so random and unexpected that everyone stopped griping, turning to look at a young man named Tyson.

"What?" someone finally asked.

"Who was the smallest person in the Book of Mormon?" Tyson repeated. "Anyone know?"

"Who?"

"Ether!"

"Ether?"

"Yeah! Because he dwelt in a *cavity!*"

Everyone groaned, and one young man even threw a marshmallow. But Tyson wasn't finished.

"Did you know what pet Lehi's family took into the wilderness?"

"They took a pet?"

"What kind of pet?"

"A dog? A cat?"

"A goat?"

"No," Tyson said with a grin. "The Lord told him to take his family and *flea!*"

Everyone groaned again. But the next minute they were sharing their favorite Mormon jokes. And it wasn't long before the rain and lightning changed from an inconvenience into an adventure.

You see, it doesn't take much to change negative attitudes into upbeat, productive ones. All it takes is a person willing to channel everyone's thoughts in a more positive direction.

You can be that person!

The next time you hear the guys moaning about a service project, get them thinking about the bright side. If they complain about the next Young Men activity, remind them that there might be doughnuts and that the Young Women might be there—*anything* to channel their thoughts in a more positive direction.

As you do, you'll make activities more fun, more productive, and more exciting for everyone. You'll be magnifying your priesthood calling. And your Heavenly Father will notice your efforts and bless you for them.

Elder H. Burke Peterson said, "A teacher has a special role in the Church. His office is a necessary appendage to the Aaronic Priesthood (see D&C 84:30). Because the office is necessary, so also is the one who fills it. The teacher must understand that *just as he needs the Church, so does the Church need him*" (*Priesthood in Action*, 101; emphasis added).

As a teacher, you *do* have an important role in the Lord's Church. So make the most of it. Help watch over the people around you, and be mindful of those who might need help or encouragement. Strengthen those you associate with. Be the battery charger that keeps your friends happy and optimistic.

Remember that one person *can* make a difference. As a teacher in the Aaronic Priesthood, you not only have the power to do that but also the responsibility.

So don't wait another second.

Start now!

How to Make a Difference Now!

☑ Decide now to be a battery charger— the person who keeps everyone happy, optimistic, and full of energy, even when the day is long and the work is hard.

☑ Look for chances to strengthen your brethren. Be on the lookout for quorum members who become tired or discouraged. *Build them up!* Look for chances to "succor the weak, lift up the hands which hang down, and strengthen the feeble knees" (D&C 81:5).

☑ Wipe moans, groans, and complaints out of your life! Then, when you hear others whining, complaining, or backbiting, change the subject. Tell a joke, share a story, or sing a song—anything to channel the conversation in a more positive direction.

☑ As you prepare the sacrament this week, remember the importance of what you're doing. Set an example of reverence and respect for the ordinance.

SEEING ANOTHER EAGLE FLY
The Power of Being a Priest

The phone was ringing when I turned off the lawn mower, and I bolted across the yard to answer it, tripping over my dog and nearly falling on the patio.

"Hello?"

"Hello, Brother Barker?"

"Yes, it is."

"Hi, this is Brian Wilson. I live down the street."

"Oh, hi, Brian," I said, catching my breath and trying not to laugh at his greeting. I *knew* who Brian was. Over the years I'd been his Scoutmaster, his algebra teacher, and his baseball coach. He was seventeen now, and he was still one of my all-time favorite young men.

"What's up?"

"I was wondering if I could ask a favor."

"Sure! What do you need?"

"You know my dad just had surgery, right?"

"Yeah."

"Well, we're supposed to go home teaching tomorrow, but he's really not ready to leave the house. I was wondering if you'd be my companion for the night."

"Yeah, sure, Brian. That'd be great. Is there anything special you need me to do?"

"Not really. I already have a lesson planned, but if you have any good thoughts or stories, you could share them."

"Okay. Sure."

"Thanks, Brother B! I'll pick you up at six."

Well, this will be different, I thought as I waited for him the next evening. *I'll be junior companion to a kid half my age!*

I was excited to be going, though. Brian was an awesome young man, and I was honored that he'd invited me.

And the families we visited were just as excited as I was. At the first home a little girl plopped onto his lap the moment he sat down, and two young boys planted themselves on both sides. They were excited to have Brian in their home, and their father didn't have to coax anyone to hang up the phone or turn off the TV once he got there.

Part of the reason, I'm sure, is that Brian was a great kid; he was fun to be around and everyone loved him. But there was more to it than that. Those families *knew* Brian cared about them. He cared enough to keep his appointment even though his father couldn't come.

Brian proved that he wasn't there because he had to be. He was there because he needed to be. And because he wanted to be.

I learned something important about home teaching that night. And it had nothing to do with Brian's lesson.

You might have become a home teacher when you were a teacher. But as a priest, you are specifically instructed "to preach, teach, expound, exhort, . . . and visit the house of each member, and exhort them to pray vocally and in secret and attend to all family duties" (D&C 20:46–47).

What an awesome responsibility! Where else in the

world are sixteen- and seventeen-year-old young men trusted to watch over people? But the real question is, do you take your assignment seriously? Or do you leave all the work to your companion? Do you truly watch over the families you're assigned to visit? Or do you wait until the last minute before making a quick visit just to get your home teaching done?

Brian understood what home teaching is all about. And he made a difference! Can you imagine the message he sent by making the effort to keep his appointments, even when his father was unable to help?

No wonder those little kids were jostling to sit by him!

But you know what the really exciting thing is? *You* can do the very same thing!

As a busy teenager, you have a lot of things competing for your attention. School, friends, jobs, sports, and family all demand enormous chunks of your time. And if you're old enough to date, you need to squeeze time for social activities into your calendar too.

Finding time to be an effective home teacher isn't easy!

But remember that home teaching is more than

simply repeating messages from the *Ensign* once a month. Your responsibilities include being the eyes and ears of your bishop, watching over certain families to be sure they're healthy and happy, and acting as a link between them and the bishop.

What an important responsibility!

Imagine someone who is struggling, suffering, or having difficulties of some kind. And suppose they didn't have a home teacher who was sensitive enough to notice. Can you imagine how a home teacher might feel if something catastrophic happened? Something the bishop might have been able to help with had the home teacher just taken the time to notice?

Don't ever let something like that happen!

I remember a great scene from the movie *Apollo 13*. After an explosion aboard the spacecraft on its way to the moon, engineers in Houston raced to find a way to bring the astronauts home safely. For a time it looked like they wouldn't succeed.

But during that uncertain time, the NASA flight director declared, "Failure is *not* an option!" Then, banging a fist on the table, he added, "We've never lost an American in space, and we're *not* going to lose one on my watch!"

Remember that this is *your* watch. With the same determination as that NASA flight director, resolve that the Lord will never, *ever,* lose anyone on *your* watch! Decide now to be a home teacher who truly watches over his families, ready to help out or alert the bishop at the first sign of trouble.

While we're talking about home teaching, there's something else you need to remember. Picture yourself, for instance, making a home teaching visit. Picture yourself sitting on the couch—a great companion beside you—teaching the gospel to a spellbound family.

Does that remind you of anything?

If that sounds like a couple of missionaries, you're exactly right. All the other blessings of home teaching aside, those monthly visits are preparing you to go into the world to teach the gospel. They're preparing you for two of the most incredible years of your life. So take advantage of that great opportunity and be the best home teacher you can be. Here are a couple of ideas for getting started.

SUPPORT YOUR COMPANION

Because you're young, you've probably been assigned to home teach with your father or another member of the Melchizedek Priesthood. Chances are, your companion already has experience as a home teacher, so follow his lead. Learn from his example.

Then be sure to make his job easier by making yourself available for visits. Take your turn making appointments, teaching lessons, and sharing thoughts and insights.

Learning to work closely with your companion as you teach the gospel will be a tremendous blessing on your mission.

HONE YOUR TEACHING SKILLS

When I was a missionary, we memorized our lessons from a discussion manual and then taught them word for word. Today missionaries learn the principles of the gospel in order to teach them in their own words.

Home teaching gives you the opportunity to practice that critical skill. So don't simply read the First

Presidency message word for word from the *Ensign*. Instead, learn to relate the message in *your own* words. Try to enrich the lesson with personal experiences, and adapt it to fit the needs of the families you teach. Find ways to include your companion, and try to involve those you're teaching. Even the little kids! Try asking such questions as "What do you think that means?" or "How do you think Nephi felt?" or "Have you ever had an experience like that?"

Home teaching is one of the closest experiences you'll ever have to actual missionary work. Take advantage of it!

LEARN TO BEAR YOUR TESTIMONY

On your mission, few things will touch and influence people as much as the power of your testimony. So you need to learn to share it *now.*

Yes, sharing deep, personal feelings can be hard for many people, and bearing your testimony might be scary. But remember that you're among friends! So open your heart and share your feelings. Learn to express your love for your Heavenly Father in front of others. Learn to put the feelings and promptings of the Spirit into words.

You have the power to be a great home teacher. You have the power to make a difference in the lives of others. You can make a difference to the families you teach, to your companion, and to those you will one day teach on your mission.

Make the most of your opportunities!

Preaching, Teaching, and Exhorting

Several years ago the young men in my ward conducted a priesthood campout. As I was helping to clean up after dinner, I noticed one of the priests—a young man named Matt—sitting with one of the deacons. I couldn't hear what they were talking about, but I could tell that Matt was excited about something. He was speaking rapidly and making enthusiastic gestures with his hands.

Probably talking about football, I thought as I wiped down a table. Matt was a receiver on the high school team, and I figured he was recounting his exploits on the field.

But a little later I saw him doing the same thing with another young man. Over the course of the weekend he worked his way through the deacons quorum and then started in on the teachers.

"What're you doing?" I asked him a little later.

"Just checking up on everyone," he said. "Just making sure they're all planning on serving missions."

"Really?"

He nodded. "Yeah. I'm just trying to pump them up a little. I make sure they're going and then tell them some of the things I'm doing to prepare for mine."

"Wow, Matt, I'm impressed."

He grinned. "Do you remember Will Anderson?"

"Will? Sure," I said, picturing a young man who had once lived in the ward. He'd moved after returning from his mission, but he'd been an outstanding role model for the youth in the neighborhood. The younger boys all idolized him.

"Will really got *me* fired up about going on a mission," Matt said. "We were out camping—just like we are now—and he got after me for not reading the Book of Mormon every day."

"And now you're doing the same thing?"

He nodded. "Will made a difference to me. And I want to do the same thing for someone else."

Encouraging young men to prepare for missions, to do their best in Scouting, and to honor and magnify their priesthood callings is the sort of thing I picture when I think of a priest's charge to "exhort."

Believe it or not, many of the young men in your ward—the teachers, deacons, and Primary boys—watch you. They watch the way you act and the way you dress. They'll do many of the things they see you do. And if you set a good example, you can have an enormous impact on how they do in school, how seriously they work in Scouts, and how strong their testimonies become.

I once heard an awesome talk at an Eagle Scout banquet. The speaker explained how newborn eagles sit in their nests and watch as their parents soar over the mountains. Eventually the day comes when the parents spread their wings and the young eagles say, "Hey, *I've* got a pair of those!"

And then the young eagles—without ever having had a lesson—spread their wings and fly.

How do they know how?

The young men in your ward—
the teachers, deacons, and Primary
boys—watch you. They watch the
way you act and the way you dress.
They'll do many of the things
they see you do. And if you set a
good example, you can have an
enormous impact on how they do
in school, how seriously they work
in Scouts, and how strong their
testimonies become.

They saw another eagle do it!

As you magnify your calling as a priest—blessing the sacrament, home teaching, and preparing for your mission—remember that other young men are watching you. You can have an impact on the way they fulfill their priesthood duties and how they one day handle the responsibility of being a priest.

And the day might come when they are able to spread their wings and soar into the heavens because they saw another eagle do it—because they saw *you* do it.

So give them a good example to look up to! Give them a good example to follow. Set your standards high, and use the power of your example to show how Aaronic Priesthood holders should act and work and talk and dress.

PREPARING FOR THE MELCHIZEDEK PRIESTHOOD

I have a young friend who plays in his high school jazz band. A district festival was coming up that featured several talented bands and a number of prestigious judges. Brandon's band had been preparing all year, but as the festival approached, the intensity of their practices increased.

"We were determined to bring the house down," he said. "So the closer we got, the harder we worked. By the last week, we were having daily rehearsals and making sure everyone had their parts down cold."

Did it work?

"Yes! I don't want to brag or anything," Brandon said. "But we rocked their socks!"

I didn't doubt it. I've done the same thing myself. Like a runner making a last, powerful kick at the end of a long race, I've made final, valiant charges right before big tests, big games, and big performances.

As a priest—and a prospective elder—you are nearing the end of your time of preparation. The time is coming closer and closer for you to receive the Melchizedek Priesthood, to be ordained an elder, and to serve your mission. But you have time to make a final, heroic effort to prepare yourself as well as you can.

Are you up for it?

Great!

Be sure that you're reading your scriptures daily. Become even closer to your Heavenly Father through sincere, heartfelt prayer. Be a faithful home teacher. Set a good example for the younger boys in the ward.

As you do, you'll discover the power of being a priest. You'll magnify your priesthood calling. You'll be able to charge into your mission with the confidence of Helaman's army. You'll be able to bless the lives of others in ways you never believed possible.

Don't wait another second!

Start now!

How to Make a Difference Now!

☑ Think now of something you could do to make yourself a better home teacher. It might be something that makes you a better companion or something special you could do for a member of the families you teach. Now do it!

☑ Be sure to take your turn presenting the home teaching message. Find ways to personalize it, and then teach it in your own words.

☑ Think of someone in your ward or school you could encourage to earn his Eagle or prepare for a mission. Do something today to follow through!

☑ Remember that younger boys in the ward are watching you. So take a good look at yourself. Are you setting a good example for them? Are you teaching them to magnify their priesthood callings and prepare for their missions? If not, start now! *Show* them how members of the Aaronic Priesthood should act and talk and dress.

FLY FISHING, CINNAMON ROLLS, AND ROCK 'N' ROLL

The Power of Preparing for Your Mission

"This is impossible!"

Elder Jackson held a sewing needle up to the light, squinting at the tiny eye like a kid inspecting a creepy garden spider. He shook his head.

"Forget camels," he said. "I can't get a single piece of *thread* through this thing."

I looked up from my desk. My companion was usually the happiest, most optimistic elder in the mission. Until that moment, I didn't know he could *be* discouraged.

"What's the matter?"

"I need to sew a new button on my shirt. But I can't thread this needle."

He held the tiny needle between two fingers, pulling a face as if it were an old, smelly sweat sock. "Elder, I'm convinced the adversary is at work here."

"You *what?*"

"Seriously, this needle's holding up the Lord's work: it's endangering the entire mission!"

I couldn't help grinning. My fun-loving companion was back to his old self again. I put my journal down and walked over. "Let me have a look."

"Good luck," he said, handing the needle over with a length of black thread. "But unless you've got eyes like Superman, you won't be able to do it."

I took the needle and had a look. Sure enough, the eye was a tiny, almost imperceptible hole.

But I'd seen worse.

I wet the end of the black thread, held the needle up to the light, and quickly slipped the thread through the eye. "There you go."

Elder Jackson's eyes popped. "What the . . . I mean, where did . . . I mean, how did you *do* that?"

I laughed and then began singing a song from the musical *Saturday's Warrior:* "I am not the ordinary, fearlessly extraordinary, needle-threading missionary, in my humble waaaay."

Elder Jackson winced (I really don't sing very well) and then spent the next couple of minutes inspecting his freshly threaded needle like a Da Vinci code breaker trying to unravel a puzzle.

I just grinned. I didn't really know much about sewing. But I did know a little bit about fly-fishing. I had experience tying itty-bitty flies to a fishing line, often when the wind was blowing and when my hands were wet, cold, and numb. Compared to some of the flies I fished with, the hole in Elder Jackson's sewing needle seemed as large as a railroad tunnel.

I never knew that fly-fishing skills would one day come in handy on my mission. If I had, I would have spent a lot more time fishing!

Actually, there are a lot of things I wish I'd spent more time doing before my mission—things like studying my scriptures, learning the gospel, and strengthening my testimony. My mission to Japan was one of the greatest experiences of my life. But looking back I wish I'd done more to prepare for those two incredible years.

That's a lesson I hope *you* don't learn the hard way!

I happen to be a junior high school teacher. I was sitting at my desk one morning when a student named Levi walked in with a plateful of homemade cinnamon rolls.

"What's the occasion, Levi?"

"No occasion. I made these for my family last night and thought you might like a couple."

"You *made* these? By yourself?"

He nodded proudly. "My mom's always teaching us how to cook and bake things. It's part of her personal 'missionary training program.'"

Wow, I thought, impressed with both Levi and his mother. And later—as I bit into one of Levi's rolls after warming it in the microwave—I thought how awesome it would be to have him as a missionary companion.

It turned out that when it came to preparing for his mission, Levi was doing more than learning to bake cinnamon rolls. His mother had taught him how to sew, wash clothes, and cook appetizing meals. His father had taught him to fix flat bicycle tires and make simple household repairs.

And that was in addition to spiritual preparation

that included family scripture study and personal reading of the Book of Mormon. I envied the elders who would one day be Levi's missionary companions. And I knew the people he taught would be in good hands.

"What we need now," Elder M. Russell Ballard said, "is the greatest generation of missionaries in the history of the Church. We need worthy, qualified, spiritually energized missionaries who, like Helaman's 2,000 stripling warriors, are 'exceedingly valiant for courage, and also for strength and activity' and who are 'true at all times in whatsoever thing they [are] entrusted'" ("Greatest Generation of Missionaries," 47).

Levi was well on his way to becoming one of those great missionaries. And the Aaronic Priesthood is preparing *you* to become part of the greatest generation of missionaries. Your priesthood callings are giving you experience in leadership, gospel study, service, and teaching. They can transform you into a dynamic, spiritually energized missionary ready to explode into the mission field.

The question is, are you doing your part?

I used to coach a Little League baseball team. Before the start of the season, we practiced nearly every day, learning to hit, throw, field, and run bases. My pitchers worked on two- and four-seam fastballs, pitching from the windup and the stretch and throwing pickoffs to all three bases. My fielders learned to pull down soaring fly balls and snatch up hard, sizzling grounders.

We didn't wait until the day before a big game to get ready. We wanted to play our best from the very first day, and we worked as hard as we could to start the season with a bang.

To be a great missionary, you need to use the same strategy. You can't wait until you receive your call. You need to start preparing now—today! Begin preparing to be a rock-'em, sock-'em, razzle-dazzle, baptize-everyone-in-sight missionary from your very first day.

"We encourage you great, young priesthood bearers to start both your temporal and spiritual preparation now to be fully worthy and ready to accept your call to wear that special badge of a full-time missionary," Elder L. Tom Perry said. "I can honestly promise you that [your mission] will be one of the great experiences of your life. It is impossible to stay even with the Lord. The more you attempt to give to Him, the more He blesses your lives, yea, even an hundredfold" ("Called to Serve," 41).

I hope you're already on your way. But let me give you a few ideas for becoming a spiritually energized missionary.

STRENGTHEN YOUR TESTIMONY

Of all the tools you'll use as a missionary, none will be as powerful or effective as your own testimony. When you are able to testify that the Church is true, the Holy Ghost will bear witness to the people you teach. Your personal testimony, along with the power of the Holy Ghost (what my seminary teacher called "the ole one-two punch"), will touch them, affect them, and convert them.

But you can't wait until you reach the mission field to build a powerful testimony. As Elder Ballard said, "This isn't a time for spiritual weaklings. We cannot send you on a mission to be reactivated, reformed, or to receive a testimony. We just don't have time for that. We need you to be filled with 'faith, hope, charity and

Of all the tools you'll use as
a missionary, none will be as
powerful or effective as your own
testimony. When you are able to
testify that the Church is true,
the Holy Ghost will bear witness
to the people you teach. Your
personal testimony, along with
the power of the Holy Ghost, will
touch them, affect them,
and convert them.

love, with an eye single to the glory of God'" ("Greatest Generation of Missionaries," 47).

So how do you learn for yourself that the gospel is true? How do you strengthen your conviction that Joseph Smith was a prophet and that The Church of Jesus Christ of Latter-day Saints is the Lord's Church upon the earth? Here are a few suggestions.

READ AND PONDER THE BOOK OF MORMON

If you haven't read the Book of Mormon, start today—right now! There's no other way to learn for yourself that it's true.

And if you *have* read it, read it again! As a missionary you'll need to *testify* that it was delivered to Joseph Smith by an angel. You'll need to testify that the Prophet translated it through the gift and power of God. You'll need to testify that it is the word of God.

Do you know that it is? If not, the key words are *read, ponder,* and *pray.* Read the Book of Mormon carefully. Think about what you're reading. And as you finish each page ask yourself, "Is this true? Could Joseph

Smith possibly have made this up? Or is it truly the work of Nephi and Alma and Moroni and Mormon?"

As you do those things, remember the next suggestion.

PRAY OFTEN

Moroni challenged those who read the Book of Mormon to ask their Heavenly Father if it is true. And he promised those who ask with a sincere heart, with real intent, and with faith in Christ that God will reveal the truth of it unto them (Moroni 10:4).

As a missionary, you'll challenge people to test that promise. So test it yourself! Learn for yourself that it works!

As you read and ponder the Book of Mormon, *pray* for a witness. Pray for it every day. Tell your Father in Heaven that you *want* a witness, that you want to *know* that the book is true. Then be patient. Keep reading. Keep praying. Have faith that your Heavenly Father will manifest the truth of the Book of Mormon to you.

Grow Close to Your Father in Heaven

Being a missionary is a lot like being on a roller-coaster. There are a lot of ups and downs. To get through the downs, you need to be close to your Heavenly Father. And the best way to develop that close relationship is to pray often.

My high school seminary teacher suggested what he called the Three-a-Day plan.

"Begin every day with prayer," he said. "Tell the Lord what you hope to accomplish that day and what help you'll need from him. Commit to doing your part and to doing your very best to be successful."

Then, sometime during the day, find time for a check-in prayer.

"Let the Lord know how you're doing," he explained. "Give thanks for help you've received, and ask for anything more you might need."

Finally, at the end of the day, comes an accountability prayer.

"Tell the Lord how you did; share your thoughts, concerns, and feelings. Give thanks for whatever help and blessings you received. And if you fell short of your expectations—if you didn't quite make your best effort—be honest and say so. Then commit to doing better tomorrow."

When you approach the Lord as a missionary—needing help finding investigators or in reaching that special family you're teaching—you'll need to know how to offer prayers that do more than bounce off the ceiling. Develop that ability now by praying sincerely and frequently.

LIVE THE COMMANDMENTS

While I was on my mission to Japan, I taught a man named Yamashita. About sixty years old, he drank tea every day, and he'd smoked from the time he was a teenager. But when we taught him the Word of Wisdom, he agreed to give up hot drinks and tobacco.

He didn't have much money, but when we challenged him to pay his tithing he said that he would.

Keep the Sabbath day holy?

No problem.

Pray?

Every day.

Attend his meetings?

Of course.

I exchanged glances with my companion. Brother Yamashita seemed like the perfect investigator. But I sensed that something was wrong, that I was missing something.

Finally I just asked him.

"Brother Yamashita, are you worthy to be baptized? Are you worthy in every way?"

He looked at the floor for several seconds and then shook his head.

"What is it?" I asked, feeling my heart drop and fearing the worst. We'd covered everything I could think of, and I couldn't imagine anything we might have missed.

Drugs?

Nah!

Alcohol?

We'd covered that.

What, then?

"Well," he began. Then he stood up. "It'll be easier if I just show you."

He was gone for a couple of minutes, finally

returning with a cardboard box. He placed it on the table and motioned for me to open it.

My heart was racing as I cast another worried look at my companion. But then I reached for the box and lifted the lid.

Records. Rock 'n' roll records—the kind we listened to before CDs and iPods were invented.

And not just rock 'n' roll but rowdy rock 'n' roll. Led Zepplin. Aerosmith. KISS. You might not recognize any of those bands, but they were big when I was a teenager. And they certainly didn't play the kind of music missionaries were allowed to listen to.

"I don't get it," I said, thumbing through albums by Deep Purple, Grand Funk Railroad, and the Doobie Brothers. "What is this?"

"My collection," he said sadly.

"Yeah, but . . ."

"I've heard that Mormons aren't allowed to listen to music like this."

It was all I could do not to laugh. I was so relieved not to be dealing with drugs, alcohol, or some serious moral transgression that I wanted to hug him. Besides, the image of this kind, elderly man rockin' out to music was silly.

"Well, we *are* encouraged to listen to uplifting, inspirational music," I said, "but none of this is going to keep you from being baptized."

Brother Yamashita kept his records boxed up anyway, proving the depth of his convictions. And when he was baptized the next week, my companion gave him a *Saturday's Warrior* album.

Many of the people you teach on your mission will have tougher challenges to overcome than Brother Yamashita's. You'll need the power of the Holy Ghost and the strength of your own testimony to help them.

The question is, will you be ready for that?

Imagine, for instance, a missionary teaching the law of tithing to someone who struggles to pay his bills or even to find enough money to feed his family. Imagine challenging him to pay his tithing by saying, "I'm pretty sure the Lord will bless you if you do."

Now imagine another missionary, this one filled with conviction, testifying with the power of the Holy Ghost, "I *know* this principle is true! I *know* that when you show your faith in the Lord—when you sacrifice and pay an honest tithe—that the Lord will open the windows of heaven and pour out a blessing such that there won't be room enough to receive it!"

There's only one way to develop a testimony like that. And that's by living the principles of the gospel. Then, when it's your turn to testify about the law of tithing, the law of chastity, the Word of Wisdom, or the Sabbath day, you won't have to say, "I'm pretty sure this is true" or "My dad really believes this."

Instead, you'll be able to say, "I *know* this is true because I have paid my tithing and lived the law of chastity and obeyed the Word of Wisdom and kept the Sabbath day holy and know from the bottom of my heart that the Lord has blessed me for it. And I know— I absolutely *know*—that the Lord will bless you too!"

Do Your Best in School

I know what you're thinking. But as a missionary you'll meet and talk with people from all walks of life. And it's important for you to be able to read, speak, and write well.

"Take your schooling seriously," Elder L. Tom

Perry counseled. To be an effective missionary, "it is important to be able to read, speak, and write with intelligence. Expand your knowledge of the world around you by reading good books. Learn how to study. Then apply your improved study habits to learning the gospel of Jesus Christ. Consistently and regularly read from the Book of Mormon" ("Raising the Bar," 48).

That's great advice! It may not seem important now, but working hard in school now will pay enormous dividends on your mission.

"[Missionary] work is rigorous," President Gordon B. Hinckley said. "It demands strength and vitality. It demands mental sharpness and capacity. It demands faith, desire, and consecration. It demands clean hands and a pure heart" ("Missionary Service," 17).

Yes, missionary work is hard. But those who do the Lord's work earn the Lord's pay. Your mission will be one of the most incredible experiences of your life. So prepare now to be an outstanding missionary. Do your best now to become part of the greatest generation of missionaries the world has ever known!

How to Make a Difference Now!

☑ Choose one thing you can do *today* that will help you to be a better missionary. Follow through and do it!

☑ Read and ponder the Book of Mormon every day! Strengthen your testimony that it truly is the word of God.

☑ Pray often. Grow close to your Heavenly Father by praying frequently and sincerely. Learn to communicate now with your Father in Heaven so you'll be able to do it later as a missionary.

☑ Live the commandments. Develop your testimony of paying tithing, living the law of chastity, obeying the Word of Wisdom, and keeping the Sabbath day holy so you'll be better able to teach those principles on your mission.

☑ Do your best in school. Expand your horizons. You never know what knowledge and experiences might one day be important on your mission, so work now to enrich yourself with as many facts, ideas, and experiences as you can.

HOW TO CLEAN A CAMPSITE
The Power of Leadership

Seventeen-year-old Trennon carefully poured a bowlful of cake batter into a waiting Dutch oven.

"Mmmm," he said, licking his lips as he spooned out the last of the batter. "This is looking good. What do you think, Bishop?"

The bishop looked over Trennon's shoulder and nodded his approval. "I'd say it looks just about right."

"Good! And now for the *pièce de resistance.*"

"*Rési*stance."

"What?"

"*Rési*stance. It's pronounced, '*pièce de rési*stance.'"

"Sorry. I'm better at Spanish. Anyway, would you hand me a can of pop?"

"Soda pop? Which flavor?"

"Do we have orange?"

"Of course."

"Then one can of orange soda, please."

Several of the deacons and teachers wandered over to watch as Trennon worked on his cobbler. The Young Men were taking part in an Aaronic Priesthood camp-out, and Trennon—as first assistant in the priests quorum—was in charge.

As the younger young men watched curiously, Trennon popped the soda can open and held it over his cobbler.

"What're you gonna do with *that?*" one of the deacons asked.

Trennon looked up, acting surprised as if just noticing that he had an audience. "What? Oh, *this?* Watch!"

With the care of a surgeon performing a delicate procedure, he poured the orange soda over the batter to create a nice, swirling design.

"Oh, yeah," he said, smacking his lips. "That looks great. What do you think, Bishop?"

"It's a masterpiece, Trennon, but how about one more little swirl right there at the top?"

"Oh," Trennon said, adding another swirl to the batter. "I can't believe I missed that! Better?"

"Perfect!"

Trennon grinned, looking up at his spellbound audience. "Those orange swirls are going to bake into the batter, so when this is done it'll look awesome! And it'll *taste* even better!"

"Who's it for?" someone finally asked.

"It's actually a prize," Trennon announced, placing a lid on the oven. He then set it on a bed of glowing coals and placed several coals on the lid.

"A prize? For what?"

"For the cleanest campsite. After dinner, Bishop Smart and I are going to inspect the camp. Whoever has the cleanest campsite gets the cobbler for dessert."

There was a sudden flurry of excited whispering. A couple of teachers standing near the back of the group exchanged glances and then bolted for their tents. A moment later everyone else was doing the same.

The bishop smiled, reaching over to clap Trennon on the shoulder.

"Well done."

"Thanks, Bishop, but the Oscar really goes to you."

By the time dinner was ready, the entire camp was as neat as a pin and cleaner than a hungry Scout's dinner plate.

Well, maybe not quite *that* clean, but you get the idea.

The important thing is that through effective leadership, Trennon was able to get a group of energetic teenagers to clean their campsites. He didn't order anyone, he didn't threaten anyone, he didn't beg anyone. As a matter of fact, he didn't even *ask* anyone! But he nevertheless got the job done.

On top of that, he turned a tedious campsite chore into an activity that was, well, *fun!*

One of the most awesome things about the Aaronic Priesthood is that it gives young men experience in leadership. You might be called to be president of your quorum, for instance. You might be called as a counselor, assistant, or secretary, or you might be called as a troop, team, or crew leader in Scouts.

Whatever the case, those callings will prepare you for even greater leadership positions in the future.

They will prepare you for leadership on your mission, in your family, in your career, and even in the Church.

Being trusted with a position of leadership is an awesome experience. But it's a great responsibility too. As a priesthood leader you're accountable for the success of your quorum and for each of its members. You are responsible for teaching quorum members their duties, helping them to become stronger in the Church, strengthening their testimony, and preparing them for the Melchizedek Priesthood.

Sound like a big job?

It is! But as you do your best to serve your quorum, your Heavenly Father will bless you and help you. And the lessons you learn will bless you throughout your life.

Remember that when you are called to be a quorum leader, the keys of leadership for the quorum are given to *you*—not to your teachers and not to your advisers. They are given to *you*.

You see, your Heavenly Father needs strong, motivated teenagers who can help other young men find their way. That's because no matter how awesome your

Your Heavenly Father needs strong, motivated teenagers who can help other young men find their way. That's because no matter how awesome your adult advisers are, there's no one who understands teenagers better than other teenagers.

adult advisers are, there's no one who understands teenagers better than other teenagers.

Think of it this way: you know what it's like being a teenager *today*. You know what it's like to deal with challenges such as Internet predators and pornography, violent video games, and inappropriate cell phone texting—things that didn't even exist when your adult leaders were your age.

And that means *you* can relate to the members of your quorum in ways that most adults can't. You can reach and influence them in ways that older leaders might never think of. And your Heavenly Father is counting on you to get the job done.

Remember that there are people in this world who need strong examples to follow. Some of them might be in your own quorum. You can be that example! You can be that leader!

Not only *can* you be, but you also *need* to be.

So what are we waiting for? Let's look at a couple of ideas for becoming an effective leader.

LEAD BY EXAMPLE

I know a young man named Dustin who was president of his teachers quorum *and* captain of his Varsity Scout team. During a presidency meeting, his adviser suggested that they get everyone to begin wearing uniforms to Scout meetings.

"How are we gonna do *that?*" Dustin asked. "I don't think anybody likes 'em."

"Then this might be a good opportunity to see how creative you can be," his adviser replied.

Dustin thought for a moment and then asked, "Are *you* going to wear one?"

"I'll buy one tomorrow."

Dustin looked at his counselors. "What about you guys?"

The counselors looked reluctant, but one of them said, "I will if you will."

Dustin nodded. And that week Dustin, his counselors, and his advisers all showed up to Scout meeting in full uniform. No one said a word about it, but the message was clear. And over the next couple of weeks the other Scouts began showing up in uniform too.

That's the power of example.

You can talk all you want about obeying the commandments, living the Word of Wisdom, and keeping the Sabbath day holy. But no lesson will ever be as effective as the power of your own example.

So if you want the members of your quorum to be on time to meetings, be sure that you're always on time yourself. If you want everyone to be reverent during the sacrament, be sure that you're reverent. Keep your scriptures or a hymnbook handy, and read them whenever you feel tempted to giggle or whisper.

Show the members of your quorum how they should behave and work, and they will follow your example.

As the Apostle Paul counseled his young friend Timothy: "Be thou an example of the believers, in word, in conversation, in charity, in spirit, in faith, in purity" (1 Timothy 4:12).

MEET THEIR NEEDS

A young friend of mine named Dylan once began taking karate lessons. It wasn't long before he was the most energetic, enthusiastic, karate-chopping kid in school.

"You're really into this, aren't you?" I asked when he showed me his newest belt.

"Yeah," he said. "It's awesome!"

"So what's the big deal? How come you're so into it?"

I was expecting him to say because it was fun or because he got to kick and pound on people. Instead, he looked at me like a missionary about to bear his testimony and said, "Because the people there make me feel important."

"Important?"

"Yeah. When I'm working out I never feel like I'm ordinary or like I'm just one of the guys. They make me feel like I'm special."

I understood that. You see, Dylan had a need to feel important. He had a need to stand out and feel special. And karate was filling that need in a way that school and Scouts didn't.

Everyone has needs, and everyone's needs are different. Some people need opportunities to be in charge. Others need chances to express themselves, make people laugh, be heroic, learn, feel smart, or be creative. Some people need lots of friends. Others need to be the center of attention. The better you're able to meet the needs of your quorum members, the more important your quorum will be to them—and the more effectively you'll be able to lead them.

When a young man named Ethan was called to be president of his teachers quorum, he wrote down the names of everyone in the quorum and listed their interests. Then, with the help of his advisers and counselors, he began devising activities that would be especially meaningful to them.

A young man named Ben, for instance, played the trumpet.

"Ask him to bring it on our next campout," someone suggested. "He could play taps when it's time for bed."

"And reveille in the morning," the quorum adviser added. (The young men rolled their eyes, and one of them even booed softly.) "We could work on the music merit badge, and maybe Ben would like to help teach it."

Next on the list was a young man everyone called "Boomer," who loved sports.

"We could go to a basketball game together," Ethan said.

"Yeah," one of his counselors agreed. "But you know what would be *really* cool?"

"What's that?"

"We could go to one of Boomer's games! You know, watch him play sometime."

"Good idea!"

And on it went. The presidency came up with activities that each young man would especially enjoy and that would help bond everyone together.

What a fantastic idea! By organizing activities around the needs of *your* quorum, you'll keep everyone involved. You'll help to fill empty areas each young man might have. You'll show them that you care. You'll give them opportunities to be important. To be the center of attention. To be important.

So do it!

Is there a member of your quorum who just *has* to be the center of attention? Put him in charge of the next activity!

Is there someone who feels left out or neglected? Base an activity around something *he* likes to do. Find ways for him to show off his talents and expertise. Let him know that the quorum is there for *him*.

And if there's someone who's too busy with sports or drama to attend your meetings, take the quorum to him! Watch him play! Watch his play! Let him see that you're interested in him.

When you begin meeting the needs of your quorum, the members will respond—even the less-active ones. The quorum will become more important to them, and they'll become more willing to help others too.

Lead as Christ Led

When I was in college I worked as a sportswriter, and I quickly learned that watching coaches was often as fun as watching the players. Some coaches were always as cool as the carbon dioxide smoke from dry ice—even in tense, emotional games. Others would stomp and scream and wave their arms, even when they were winning.

You've probably had leaders who've done the same thing.

Think for a minute of leaders *you've* responded to. Chances are they weren't effective because they shouted or yelled a lot. Instead, they probably found ways to make you feel needed and important. They found ways to make you feel good about yourself, motivating you, inspiring you, and bringing out the best in you.

That's the way the Savior led.

Is there any question what kind of leader *you* should be?

Elder M. Russell Ballard once told a story about a man trying to lead a colt. The man attached a halter to the horse and pulled. The colt wouldn't budge. The man pulled harder and the horse dug in its heels. The harder the man pulled, the more firmly the horse resisted. Finally, instead of standing in front of the horse and pulling, he tried walking *alongside* the colt. Only then did the animal respond ("One More," 71).

Many young men are like that colt. If you try dragging them along, they'll resist. But if you put your arm around them and walk *with* them, they'll respond.

Keep that in mind as you develop your own leadership style.

Show Them That You Care

I remember talking with a young man named Jantzen, who was an assistant to the bishop in his priests quorum.

"We challenged the elders to a golf tournament a couple of months ago," he told me. "But a guy named Mike didn't want to participate."

"He didn't like golf?"

"He *couldn't* golf. We'd all gone out once before, and he was awful. Half the time he'd swing and miss the ball. And whenever he *did* connect, he'd either slice it so bad everyone ducked, or he'd only hit it a couple of feet. Anyway, he didn't want to play because he didn't want to look dumb in front of the elders."

I couldn't blame him. But Jantzen *wanted* Mike to play. So one day he took him to the local driving range and taught him to hit simple tee shots.

"Then we went and spent a couple of hours goofing around on the chipping and putting range," he said. "It was a blast! And by the time we were done he was hooked. He realized that you don't have to play like a pro to have fun."

On top of that, Jantzen paired himself up with Mike the evening of the tournament. And he made sure the elders in their foursome were out to have fun and not worried about proving what awesome golfers they were.

But the most important thing was that Jantzen showed how much he *cared*. He proved that he was more concerned about Mike than about golf. And that's what made the difference.

I used to coach a young man named Jeff, who was the quarterback of our seventh-grade football team. He wasn't the biggest player on the team, he wasn't the fastest, and he wasn't the most athletic.

But he *was* an outstanding leader.

During practice he'd talk with his running backs and receivers, making sure they were all communicating effectively. He'd talk to his linesmen, letting them know exactly what he needed from them.

But the most impressive thing he did was to show every player that he cared about them. Whenever a receiver dropped a pass, Jeff was the first one to assure him that it didn't matter. Whenever a running back missed a hole, got tackled, or fumbled the ball, Jeff was the first one telling him not to worry about it. He'd slap him on the helmet, tell him to forget it, and then get him back in the game.

One day I showed up early to practice and found Jeff throwing passes to a receiver who struggled catching the ball.

"What's going on?" I asked.

"We're just working on our timing," Jeff said. "I've been messing up, and Marshall's helping me work out the kinks."

As if Jeff were the problem!

Those players quickly learned that Jeff was more concerned about *them* than in scoring touchdowns or winning games. The result was that those kids played their hearts out for him. Offensive linemen *exploded* into defenders who were bigger and stronger. Receivers leaped that extra inch to catch passes. Running backs fought tooth and nail for every last foot of grass they could get.

Just for Jeff.

When the members of your quorum learn that *you* care—that you really care—about them, they'll respond. They'll be more willing to follow you up the next hill. They'll be more willing to put in that extra hour of service. They'll be more willing to sit through that extra planning meeting.

And half your work will be done.

As a leader in the Aaronic Priesthood, you have the power to bless lives and inspire souls. You have the power to shape young men, keeping them spiritually healthy and pointed in the right direction.

You can do more than simply place their hands on the iron rod—you can walk beside them, jog beside them, propelling them along and placing them on a straight course to the celestial kingdom.

So take your job seriously! As you do, you'll prepare yourself for even greater, more fantastic leadership positions in the future. And you'll grow and magnify your priesthood calling more powerfully than you could ever dream possible!

How to Make a Difference Now!

☑ Think of something your quorum needs to get done. Then try to find a creative way to get everyone excited about it!

☑ Be sure to set the right example. Be positive in everything you do. Be a leader quorum members can look to when they need a good example to follow.

☑ Think of a great leader or teacher you've had. Try to think of something you especially enjoyed or appreciated about that person. See if there's someway you can use that quality in *your* quorum.

☑ Think of someone in your quorum who might be struggling. Think of something you can do to help him, bolster him, or fill some hole in his life. Now do it!

WINNING GAMES
AND ROCKING PHILISTINES
The Power of the Aaronic Priesthood

"Twenty-four to six!" the team captain bellowed, lurching as he clomped down the isle of the bus. He was clapping teammates on the shoulders, giving high fives and bumping fists with players up and down the bus. "Who's number one?"

"We are!"

"Who's number one?"

"WE ARE! WE ARE! WE ARE!"

The bus rocked as the high school football players shouted and cheered, celebrating a decisive victory over a rival team. The game had ended more than an hour before, but everyone was still crackling with the energy that comes after a big win.

Seventeen-year-old Justin was caught up in the excitement, punching, wrestling, and high-fiving his teammates. He was sticky with Gatorade (he'd been standing too close to the coach when the team doused him), but he'd caught two passes in the game, taking one of them nearly thirty yards before being tackled, setting up the team's first touchdown.

It was the team's best game of the season.

Justin celebrated with his teammates, but when the excitement finally died a little, he returned to his seat at the back of the bus. Two players were in the seat just ahead of him, sitting with their heads together. Justin couldn't help but see what they were doing, and what he saw shocked him.

The players were looking at a cell phone. And the images they were looking at would have gotten them both suspended from the team and probably from school.

"Knock that off," Justin said, speaking just loud enough for the two players to hear.

"Or what?" one of the players growled back. "What are you gonna do?"

"You really want to find out?" Justin asked. "Or would you rather just turn off the phone?"

The two young men exchanged angry glances, mumbling and muttering under their breath, but they turned off the phone.

Later—after the bus had arrived at the school and everyone was gathering up their gear—the two confronted Justin.

"You better not be thinking about telling the coach," one of them said. The two were standing shoulder to shoulder as if trying to intimidate Justin, but he stood his ground.

"I don't think the coach should be your biggest concern," he said.

"Why not?"

"Because I've heard you talk in seminary," Justin said. "I've heard you bear your testimony. What do you think Brother Nielsen would say about your little hobby?"

Justin turned to the second player. "Think your mother would be proud? Or your little sisters?"

Neither one replied. But a day or two later, the first young man came looking for Justin in the locker room.

"Can we talk for a minute?" he asked. "Outside?"

Justin nodded. They left the locker room and began walking around the track.

"I just wanted to apologize for the other night," he said. "I was wrong, and I know it."

"It's no big deal."

"No, it *is* a big deal. The thing is, I don't know why you mentioned Brother Nielsen, but . . . well, that kind of shook me up."

"Why's that?"

The young man looked away for a moment. "About a week ago I was talking with him. He told me how proud he was of me. And he told me what a good example I am." He shook his head. "So it really hit me hard when you mentioned him. I realized I was letting him down. I realized I was letting a lot of people down."

He stopped and shook Justin's hand. "Anyway, I wanted to apologize and say thanks for setting me straight."

I was proud of Justin for doing what he did. If you've ever been in a similar situation, you know how hard it can be speaking up, especially when it involves friends or teammates.

It wasn't easy for Justin. But he knew something important: your Heavenly Father blesses those who choose the right. He rewards those who put their trust in him.

As the Lord once said to Hyrum Smith, "Put your trust in that Spirit which leadeth to do good—yea, to do justly, to walk humbly, to judge righteously; and this is my Spirit . . . which shall fill your soul with joy" (D&C 11:12–13).

When I was in seminary, our teacher told us the story of David and Goliath.

"Can you even *picture* this giant?" Brother Miller asked. "Scholars say he was nine, ten, maybe even eleven feet tall."

He pointed toward the ceiling. "If Goliath was just ten feet tall, not only would he not fit in this room, but his head and shoulders would be poking two or three *feet* through the top of the ceiling as well!"

We all looked up, trying to picture someone that big.

"Goliath was so big that his armor alone weighed

more than a hundred twenty pounds," he said, "and the top of his spear weighed almost twenty pounds."

Brother Miller explained that Goliath knew he was invincible, and like many bullies he couldn't resist taunting his enemies. Every morning he stormed onto the plain between the warring armies, taunting the Israelites and daring them to fight.

"You need to remember that the Israelites weren't a bunch of cupcakes," Brother Miller continued. "They had champions of their own. But none of them dared to face Goliath. As the scripture says, 'All the men of Israel, when they saw the man, fled from him, and were sore afraid'" (1 Samuel 17:24).

Our teacher explained that this went on for forty days. And then David showed up to visit his brothers. He heard Goliath's challenge and was amazed that no one was willing to go against him. So David decided to take on the monster himself.

"He wasn't scared?" someone asked.

"Maybe he *was* scared," a young woman named Sariah suggested. "But he had faith. He knew that God would protect him."

"I think that's it exactly," Brother Miller said. "David

had faith in his Heavenly Father. He'd been in tough spots before, and the Lord had always delivered him."

"What kind of tough spots?" someone asked.

"He killed a lion," a young man named Sean answered. "He killed a lion and he killed a bear trying to take lambs from his father's flock."

"Really?"

Brother Miller nodded, reading again from 1 Samuel 17: "David said moreover, The Lord that delivered me out of the paw of the lion, and out of the paw of the bear, he will deliver me out of the hand of this Philistine" (v. 37).

"You see," Brother Miller said, "David knew the Lord had protected him before. And he knew the Lord would help him again."

Brother Miller closed his book. "I've always loved that story," he said. "But have you ever wondered why it's important?"

No one answered. Over the years, though, I've often thought about David and Goliath. And I believe there are two important lessons in that story. The first is that the Lord blesses those who put their trust in him. Whether they're choosing the right in a difficult situation, paying their tithing when they don't have much money, or risking criticism by walking out of an inappropriate movie, the Lord rewards those who do what's right.

To explain the second lesson, I need to ask a question: Where do you think David learned to use a sling?

The scriptures don't tell us, but today that's the sort of thing a young man might learn in Scouts. That's the sort of thing a young man might learn through activities in the Aaronic Priesthood.

You see, you're going to face Goliaths in your life too. You're going to face dangers, challenges, trials, and obstacles that will seem every bit as big and formidable as Goliath seemed to David.

But the Aaronic Priesthood provides you with the spiritual weapons you'll need to face Goliaths and to overcome them. And the more you honor your priesthood—the better you magnify your callings—the more powerful those spiritual weapons will be.

Elder Joseph B. Wirthlin said, "I want to tell you young men that the Lord has His eye upon you. He loves you. He knows you. He knows your triumphs and your trials, your successes and your heartaches.

The Aaronic Priesthood provides
you with the spiritual weapons
you'll need to face Goliaths and
to overcome them. And the more
you honor your priesthood—
the better you magnify your
callings—the more powerful
those spiritual weapons will be.

"He knows that at times you may look at the challenges you may face and may think they're too big to handle. He is, however, willing and ready to help you as you grow into the men you are to become" ("Growing into the Priesthood," 39).

Remember that when you put your trust in the Lord, you qualify for great blessings. As you honor your priesthood, you become eligible for the companionship of the Holy Ghost. Not only that, but the Aaronic Priesthood that you bear "holds the keys of the ministering of angels" (D&C 13:1).

What does that mean?

It means you are entitled to divine help as you face the challenges of life. You might never have an angel appear before you, taking you by the hand and leading you through difficulties. But you are still entitled to guidance and inspiration when you need it.

And not just at church. When you honor your priesthood, you are entitled to guidance at home, at work, at school, and in whatever righteous activities you're involved in, including music, drama, debate—even sports!

There was a time when the village of the Old

Testament prophet Elisha was surrounded by a mighty Syrian army. Fearing the people were about to be conquered, a servant exclaimed, "Alas, my master! how shall we do?"

Elisha answered, "Fear not: for they that be with us are more than they that be with them.

"And Elisha prayed, and said, Lord, I pray thee, open his eyes, that he may see. And the Lord opened the eyes of the young man; and he saw: and behold, the mountain was full of horses and chariots of fire round about Elisha" (2 Kings 6:15–17).

You might never see those angels. But if you're living as your Heavenly Father expects you to, then when Goliath-like challenges threaten to bring you down, you can rest assured that the angels are there!

As a member of the Aaronic Priesthood, you have one of the greatest blessings a young man could ever have. You have the power and authority of your Father in Heaven to act in his name and bless the lives of others.

You already know that it's not enough to simply have that power. Your Heavenly Father expects you to use it. To make the most of it. And to make a difference with it.

The Lord once said: "I know thy works, that thou art neither cold nor hot: I would thou wert cold or hot. So then because thou art lukewarm, and neither cold nor hot, I will spue thee out of my mouth" (Revelation 3:15–16).

In those verses I believe the Lord is pleading with you to stand up and make a difference. He is pleading with you to do more than sit on the back row, half-heartedly living the gospel.

He is pleading with you to do your best, to stand tall, and to lengthen your stride. He is pleading with you to magnify your calling and become the outstanding young man you were sent here to be.

Are you up to the challenge?

If you are, then I can testify that you will qualify, as Jesus said, for "all that my Father hath" (D&C 84:38), which is eternal life in the kingdom of God.

And at the completion of your mission on this earth, you will have the privilege of having your Heavenly Father wrap his arms around you and say,

"Well done, thou good and faithful servant" (Matthew 25:21).

Now's your chance.

Go do it!

How to Make a Difference Now!

☑ Remember the words "Trust in the Lord" (Psalm 37:3; Proverbs 3:5). Anytime you struggle with a decision or need a shot of faith, remember those words: "Trust in the Lord."

☑ Remember that there is a spiritual reason for everything you do in the Aaronic Priesthood. Every lesson, activity, and project strengthens your spiritual muscles. And every lesson, activity, and project provides you with spiritual stones and slings for the Goliaths you'll face in life.

☑ Think of one thing you can do now to strengthen yourself, build your testimony, or bless another person. Now go do it!

SOURCES

Ballard, M. Russell. "The Greatest Generation of Missionaries." *Ensign,* Nov. 2002, 46–49.

———. "One More." *Ensign,* May 2005, 69–71.

———. "Prepare to Serve." *Ensign,* May 1985, 41–43.

The Boy Scout Handbook. 10th ed. Irving, Tex.: Boy Scouts of America, 1990.

Eyring, Henry B. "A Priesthood Quorum." *Ensign,* Nov. 2006, 43–45.

Faust, James E. "A Royal Priesthood." *Ensign,* May 2006, 50–53.

Fulfilling My Duty to God: For Aaronic Priesthood Holders. Salt Lake City: The Church of Jesus Christ of Latter-day Saints, 2010.

SOURCES

Hales, Robert D. "To the Aaronic Priesthood: Preparing for the Decade of Decision." *Ensign,* May 2007, 48–51.

Hinckley, Gordon B. "Missionary Service." *First Worldwide Leadership Training Meeting,* Jan. 11, 2003, 17–21.

———. "Welfare Responsibilities of the Priesthood Quorums." *Ensign,* Nov. 1977, 84–86.

Holland, Jeffrey R. "'Sanctify Yourselves.'" *Ensign,* Nov. 2000, 38–40.

Monson, Thomas S. "Examples of Righteousness." *Ensign,* May 2008, 65–68.

———. "How Firm a Foundation." *Ensign,* Nov. 2006, 62–69.

———. "To Learn, to Do, to Be." *Ensign,* Nov. 2008, 60–68.

Nelson, Russell M. "Personal Priesthood Responsibility." *Ensign,* Nov. 2003, 44–47.

Perry, L. Tom. "Called to Serve." *Ensign,* May 1991, 39–41.

———. "Raising the Bar." *Ensign,* Nov. 2007, 46–49.

Peterson, H. Burke. *Priesthood in Action.* Salt Lake City: New Era, 1986.

Priesthood. Salt Lake City: Deseret Book, 1981.

Wirthlin, Joseph B. "Growing into the Priesthood." *Ensign,* Nov. 1999, 38–41.

ABOUT THE AUTHOR

Shane Barker's understanding of young people comes from many years of serving as an adviser in his ward's deacons and priests quorums, running Boy Scout summer camps, and working as a junior high school math teacher. He is an avid skier and snowboarder and is an active member of the National Ski Patrol. He is the author of *The Stripling Warrior and Warriorette Workout, Youth Leading Youth,* and *Be the Hero of Your Own Life Story.* Brother Barker served a mission to Japan for The Church of Jesus Christ of Latter-day Saints and is a graduate of Brigham Young University. He resides in Orem, Utah.